PRESENTS

THE COLLEGE PLAYBOOK

D1404180

Written by Lucas Spielfogel

Inquiries concerning this publication should be mailed to:

MasteryPrep
7117 Florida Blvd.
Baton Rouge, LA 70806

MasteryPrep is a trade name and/or trademark of Ring Publications LLC.

10 9 8 7 6 5 4 3 2 1

ISBN-13: 978-1-948846-70-7

Table of Contents

Getting Started

Why You Should/Should Not Listen to Me

Hey guys,

Hope all is well. My name is Lucas Spielfogel, and I appreciate you taking time to see what this book is all about. In my opinion, it's filled with advice and resources that can help you reach your college dreams, but it doesn't matter what I think. What matters is that you think my advice and resources are worth spending a bunch of time with. So, why should you listen to me?

Let's start with why you shouldn't. When I was going through the college process, I had a lot of advantages most kids don't. I went to a private high school with its own college counseling department. I'm also a third-generation college student, whereas many students— perhaps even you—are <u>striving</u> to be the first in their families to attend college. And while most American students and families are very concerned about how they'll pay for college, my family could afford it without financial aid. There's a good chance I haven't walked in your shoes, and there will be times throughout this book when you'll think, "Yah, easy for him to say." And you will be right. Why share all this? Because if I'm asking you to pour your heart and sweat into this process, the least I owe you is full honesty.

Don't be alarmed: there are some reasons you *should* listen to me. Since 2013, I have worked as executive director of the Baton Rouge Youth Coalition (BRYC), an after-school program in Baton Rouge, Louisiana, that helps high-achieving, under-resourced high school students get into, pay for, and succeed in college. Again, I haven't walked my students' paths, but I've walked arm in arm with hundreds of them through the college process: studying for the ACT, staying up all night writing essays, stressing over financial aid forms, picking the right school, and physically <u>transitioning</u> to college. It's been a grind but, working together, we've seen huge success. Eighty percent of our 300 alumni have graduated, or are on track to graduate, from more than 50 colleges across more than 20 states. They've blazed a trail for our 200 high school students—and the many more to come—who are working toward similar and greater heights. Along the way, I've gotten good at this college process thing. It's tough but beatable. Just ask my students. This book is a <u>compilation</u> of the information we at BRYC pester our students with daily. I'll tell you what we tell them, a truth you may be tired of hearing: you'll get out exactly what you put in.

Speaking of which, there's no clear-cut way to use this book. The chapters and sections build on each other, but I'll warn you: if you read the whole thing at once, you might want to cry. I suggest reading a section here, a chapter there, and referring back to parts you find helpful as you navigate high school and the college application process. Make it work for you.

Oh, two more things. Throughout the book, and in this very section, you'll notice some underlined words—there are definitions to these words in the Glossary at the back of the book. Building your vocabulary is key! Second thing: all the helpful "tools" I refer to throughout the book can be found at www.masteryprep.com/cpb-resources. The password is *CollegeSuccess*.

So, what do you say? Are you with me?

Why You Should Earn a Four-Year College Degree

People question if <u>pursuing</u> a four-year college degree (aka a bachelor's degree) is worth it. Their concerns are legit. Students will <u>willingly</u> <u>incur</u> the <u>exorbitant</u> cost of four-year college because they expect that having a bachelor's degree will lead to the jobs they want. This is partly true, partly false. Many new graduates struggle to find employment, often because what they learn in college turns out not to be useful in professional settings. Other <u>factors</u>, like race and class, have a big impact on job <u>attainment</u>, too. Any way you slice it, a four-year degree is not the one-way ticket to our dreams they told us it was.

So, what's the answer? Is a bachelor's worth it? In a word, yes. The average four-year college graduate makes a lot more money over her lifetime than the average high school graduate. And, on paper, she's qualified for many more job opportunities. That's the point: a bachelor's degree is *not* a one-way ticket to our dreams; it's the minimum to get our foot in the door.

If you want a job that will lead to more money, responsibility, and career options, a bachelor's degree is a must. Employers with <u>full-salaried</u> job openings won't give your application a second look without one.

Cool, so, a bachelor's gets your foot in the door. What gets you the job you hoped your degree would lead to? These things matter: who you know and what you look like. But you have limited control there.

What is in your control? How can you <u>ensure</u> your bachelor's is worth it? First, aim to attend a good college. We will talk more about what that means later, and my hope is this book will help with that. Second, and more important, go hard in college. Take it seriously. Take <u>rigorous</u> courses. Get involved outside of class. Learn how to work hard, communicate effectively, think creatively, and be a good teammate. This is what employers look for; I know because I am one. If you spend college slacking, your degree will be empty and not worth the paper it's printed on.

There's an old saying: "All that glitters is not gold." Four-year degrees glitter. They jump off your resume and shout, "I finished college!" loud enough to <u>pique</u> an employer's curiosity. But are you solid gold? Regardless of which college <u>conferred</u> it, does your degree represent the skills and knowledge that will make my company better? That's what we, employers, ask ourselves before making any hire.

This book is geared toward students pursuing four-year college, and I stand by my claim that a bachelor's degree is the most reliable launchpad to a long, prosperous career. But it is not the only path available after high school. In "Options Besides Four-Year College," we will talk about when community college or trade school is the best choice and the great opportunities these paths can lead to.

Options Besides Four-Year College

I hate when people tell me "college isn't for everyone." They're usually not talking about their own kids. Here's a better statement: four-year college isn't where all students will be most successful.

Not everyone will go to a four-year college. Here are some reasons why:

- Could not afford four-year college without taking on crazy <u>debt</u>.
- Don't need a bachelor's to pursue dream career.
- Need to get stronger academically before transferring to a four-year college.
- Have only had bad experiences with school and need a break.

Here are five postsecondary (post-high school) <u>alternatives</u> to four-year college:

Option One: Community College

Did you know almost half of American students in higher education attend a community college? Indeed, community college is an affordable alternative that can lead to a ton of great jobs. Community college offers students two main pathways:

Transfer to a four-year college: Many students <u>ultimately</u> want to get their bachelor's degrees but aren't ready—academically or financially—for a four-year college. In this case, community college can be a great first step, one many of my own students have taken. In community college you can <u>obtain</u> a transfer associate degree, then apply to a four-year school. In the process, you can save money and <u>shore</u> up any academic weak spots.

Get straight to work: In community college, you can also earn an <u>occupational</u> associate degree, which <u>enables</u> you to start working immediately in a specific field. Below are some examples of well-paying jobs that require an associate degree. Next to each is the average salary as it was in 2017.

- Mechanical engineering technician ($58,180)
- Cardiovascular technologist/technician ($57,250)
- Physical therapist assistant ($57,620)
- Geological and petroleum technician ($63,450)

- Occupational therapy assistant ($59,470)
- Radiologic technologist ($60,320)
- Avionics technician ($63,650)
- Electrical and electronics drafter ($63,720)
- Electrical and electronics engineering technician ($64,290)
- Computer network support specialist ($67,510)
- Engineering technician ($60,550)
- Aerospace engineering technician ($71,340)
- Web developer ($74,110)
- Magnetic resonance imaging technologist ($70,490)
- Registered nurse ($73,550)
- Diagnostic medical sonographer ($73,200)
- Funeral service manager ($93,090)
- Nuclear technician ($80,000)
- Dental hygienist ($74,680)

Option Two: Vocational or Trade School

A vocational or trade school helps students build skill sets needed for specific jobs. Below are some examples of well-paying jobs that require a vocational or trade school certificate. Next to each is the average salary as it was in 2017.

- Aircraft mechanic ($62,540)
- Insurance appraiser for automobile damage ($64,680)
- Commercial pilot ($89,350)
- Firefighting supervisor ($79,430)
- Nuclear medicine technologist ($77,660)
- Radiation therapist ($85,190)
- Construction manager ($101,000)
- Air traffic controller ($120,260)

Option Three: Military

For students not interested in continuing school, joining the Armed Forces is an <u>honorable</u> pathway that offers many benefits, including but not limited to:

- Strong starting salaries and opportunities for <u>advancement</u>
- Full medical insurance coverage for you and your family
- Technical training in a variety of fields
- Leadership experience you can use to find jobs after the military
- Financial support for college after the military
- One of the best <u>pension</u> (retirement) packages around

Option Four: Volunteer

A one- or two-year volunteer commitment after high school can be a fun and meaningful way to give back while gaining skills and experiences that can make you a more competitive candidate for jobs and college admissions in the future. Visit www.nationalservice.gov for more information.

Option Five: Gap Year

A gap year is a year off after high school. Maybe you didn't get into a four-year college, or at least not the one you wanted to attend. Maybe you need a break. Maybe you have to deal with some personal stuff. In these and other cases, a gap year can be a solid option. You can get a job, focus on personal growth or maybe take another stab at the college application process without the pressure of high school on your back. If you do take a gap year, don't let yourself drift off course. Creating a routine and setting goals will be key.

I Could Lie or Tell You Reading Is Important

I bet your school has at least one corny reading initiative. Am I right? You hate it. Am I right? It's okay. I know I am.

I was once a teacher who tried, along with my coworkers, to convince middle-schoolers to read books by telling them "readers are leaders." I converted a handful, but the rest rolled their eyes. We couldn't inspire them to do the thing I most want my own children to: read voraciously.

Growing up I found reading painfully boring, and that was before social media. I'd bet the advent of Twitter (which I love) and "the Gram" haven't increased the average American high school student's attention span. We educators are losing this war of words. #crap

Nine years in, I'm still fighting the good fight, the uphill battle to get my students to read. Magazine and newspaper articles, books, the Bible, *anything*. I beg you to consider the best advice this book has to offer: Lebron James is the GOAT.

Just kidding...that advice is to READ!

Many of my students tell me they read to escape, to take a mental respite from the stress of their everyday lives. If this resonates with you, you're probably already an avid reader, and I'm preaching to the choir. If it doesn't, here are five facts about reading that might convince you:

1. **Reading is the #1 way to improve your ACT®/SAT® score:** The ACT and SAT are reading tests. How well you do on them depends on your vocabulary, comprehension, and reading speed. You can grow all three by reading on your own. As you will learn later in this book, strong ACT/SAT scores are critical for getting into four-year colleges and earning major scholarships.

2. **Reading helps you code-switch:** Did you know there are dozens of varieties of the English language, each with its own grammar rules? In other words, Americans in different parts of the country and who represent different races speak English in different ways. Less educated folks call this "slang," but these are legitimate languages. The ACT and SAT, however, are written in Standard Written English. (So are many American books and articles.) Students who grew up speaking a dialect that's much different from Standard Written English are constantly "code-switching" between the variety of English they commonly speak

and the one that appears on standardized tests. By reading <u>consistently</u> on your own, you will begin to master the rules of Standard Written English, which will positively impact your ACT/ SAT scores, increasing your chances of getting into a good college and securing scholarships.

3. **Reading improves your writing:** Essays are <u>critical</u> in the college and scholarship application process. There are two ways to improve your writing: read more and write more. "Well-written" books and articles are <u>models</u> that you can learn from and eventually <u>inject</u> your own style into.

4. **Reading prepares you for college:** Your college professors will expect you to read hundreds more pages per week than your high school teachers do. Most college freshman struggle academically because this shift hits them like a ton of bricks. The more reading you do now, the better prepared you will be to perform well in college courses.

5. **Reading grows your brain:** Your brain is just like your body: how much you exercise it will determine how well it functions. Reading is a workout for your brain. Just as lifting weights grows your muscles, reading improves your memory and mental sharpness.

I hope one of these five facts motivates you! There's no getting around required reading for specific classes, but reading for pleasure—books, magazine articles, blog posts—will help you achieve the results I described above. If reading *isn't* enjoyable, it's either because you haven't found a genre or topic that interests you or because you don't read enough. It can take time to find out what you like to read, and like any other skill, reading takes time to master. Even thirty minutes a night can make a difference. And, guess what? You just might enjoy it.

You Need a Mentor

If you've ever walked around with a blindfold on, you know how scary it can be. You slowly inch forward with your arms <u>outstretched</u>, trying not to slam into anything. It goes better when you have someone guiding you, helping with each step.

The college process is really hard, guys. Since you haven't been through it before, it will be very much like trying to <u>navigate</u> a maze with a blindfold on. I <u>implore</u> you to find a guide before you begin slamming into things.

That guide is called a <u>mentor</u>, someone you look up to who has been where you want to go and can help you get there. A great mentor for the college process is:

- A college graduate—has walked the path you want to take
- Organized—can help you stay on top of deadlines and assignments
- A solid writer—can help with the written <u>components</u> of your application
- Dependable—follows through on commitments
- Honest—tells you what you need to hear, even when it's hard
- Steady—stays positive and calm, even when things are tough
- Resourceful—good at finding answers when something is unclear
- Trustworthy—listens with an open ear and heart, and honors <u>confidentiality</u>

It's equally important to know what a mentor is **not**:

- Guardian—replacement for parents
- Provider—source of money
- Savior—answer to all your problems
- Friend—someone you can treat as a peer

There's a good chance you're like most of my students—and most people, in general— meaning you would find it super awkward to recruit a mentor out of the blue. Where do you even begin?

Step 1: Eat humble pie: Recognize that, no matter how capable you are, your college application process will go much better if you have help. I'm 31 years old, and I have, like, a zillion mentors.

Step 2: Identify 2–3 <u>prospects</u>: Find two or three adults in your life that check the boxes on the first list above. They can (but don't have to) be people you are already close with. They definitely should not be strangers, unless you're part of a program that safely matches you with a background-checked volunteer.

Step 3: Talk to your family: Tell your parents you want a mentor for the college process. Describe your prospects. It's <u>crucial</u> your parents feel comfortable with any adult you will be spending time with.

Step 4: Make the ask: Asking someone to be your mentor may feel awkward, but the worst that could happen is the person says no. You may find it easier to send an email. It could read something like this:

Dear Mr. Howard,

As you may know, I am getting ready to begin my college application process, and I know I will need a lot of guidance. After a lot of thought and talking to my family, I am writing to officially ask if you would be my college mentor for the next year. You are someone I look up to who has walked the path I want to walk.

If you say yes, I would like to meet with you to talk about what I want to accomplish and when and where we should have our meetings. I know this is sort of out of the blue. I appreciate you giving this some thought, and I look forward to hearing back from you.

Sincerely,

Lucas

You and your mentor should start out meeting weekly for about an hour. As the college process continues, you can decide when it makes sense to have shorter or longer sessions, or when you need to meet more or less <u>frequently</u>. The information in this book should help you set up a plan for how you and your mentor will approach the process.

Your parents or a trusted relative should attend the meetings (even if they don't participate) until they feel comfortable with and fully trust your mentor. It's best to have your meetings in places where other people are, such as school, a coffee shop, or the library. Especially at the beginning, put safety first.

I'm aware I'm asking you to step way outside your comfort zone here. I wouldn't ask if I wasn't sure it's the right advice. Our high school seniors at BRYC would tell you their college mentors are <u>vital</u> to their success, and I can tell you that, without professional mentors, I would have failed a long time ago. Think about it.

In Summary...

- The college process is tough but beatable.

- To be considered for most full-salaried jobs, you must have at least a bachelor's (four-year) degree. But the value of your degree will depend on how hard you work in college—both in and outside the classroom.

- For many reasons, four-year college may not be the right fit for you, but there are many other strong postsecondary options.

- Reading consistently is one of the best decisions you can make. It will have a positive impact on your SAT/ACT score, school grades, writing ability, and life in general.

- Having a mentor is important during any phase of life. It is particularly important during the college process, which is very tough to navigate alone.

Getting and Staying on Track

What Colleges Are Looking For - The Big Five

There are five main things that will make you a strong college applicant. Let's call them the "Big Five." Not all colleges care about these things or care about them equally.

1. Grades & Course Rigor

Colleges want to see consistently strong grades or, second best, that your grades improve over the course of high school. They also want to see that you have challenged yourself by taking the hardest courses (Honors, AP, IB, etc.) you could handle. Colleges would rather see slightly lower grades in tougher courses than straight As in easy ones. Of course, they would really like to see straight As in tough ones!

Who cares? All colleges care about your grades and course rigor. More selective colleges will have higher expectations.

2. ACT/SAT Scores

These are very important. Colleges use ACT/SAT scores to see how you compare to students nationally and how ready you are for college-level work. Some colleges require SAT II Subject Tests, but we'll discuss this more later.

Who cares? Almost all colleges care about ACT/SAT scores. More selective colleges will expect higher scores. Some colleges do not require ACT/SAT scores. To learn more about that, visit www.fairtest. org.

3. Essays

Many colleges require applicants to write essays, which is your chance to flaunt your writing skills and tell your story. Your essays show that you are far more than a bunch of letters and numbers.

Who cares? Usually colleges that are smaller and more selective require essays. If essays are required, it means they matter a lot.

4. Involvement

Colleges are looking for students who have been heavily involved in 2–3 activities outside of class. "Activities" include sports, clubs, jobs, internships, and family responsibilities. It's especially awesome if you maintain your commitment to these activities over the course of a few years, and it's even better if, by the end of high school, you hold leadership roles.

Who cares? Almost all colleges like to see that you have been involved in something outside of class because it means you will enrich a campus community. As with essays, smaller, more selective colleges care more about involvement in activities.

5. Recommendation Letters

Most colleges require applicants to secure letters of recommendation from coaches, teachers, etc. Strong rec letters can set you apart, and we'll talk more later about how to get them.

Who cares? The majority of colleges care about recommendation letters. Smaller, more selective colleges care about them the most.

6. Bonus - Demonstrated Interest

"Demonstrated interest" is how much you show you want to attend a certain college. For more on this, see the article that's imaginatively titled, "Demonstrate Interest."

Race and Socioeconomic Status Play a Role

Race and financial status play a role in the college application process. There are many reasons for this, but we will focus on two. First, colleges recognize that students learn more when they are surrounded by diverse peers and challenged to consider perspectives different from their own. Second, because a bachelor's degree is the most reliable ticket to a prosperous career, colleges have a responsibility to drive social change by ensuring equal access. Most have a lot of catching up to do. For centuries students of color and low-income students have been unable to enjoy the sorts of postsecondary opportunities their wealthier and/or white peers have widely had access to. Colleges and other organizations are being more intentional to change this reality and level the playing field. We will discuss this more later, but it is important for applicants of color and/or low-income applicants to be aware of scholarships and other unique opportunities designed specifically to support them in entering, paying for, and persisting in college.

Grade-Specific Timelines

	9th Grade: Set the Tone	
	Time-Sensitive	**Ongoing**
Summer	• Stay busy: participate in a summer program you're passionate about • Read 2–3 books	• Read a book every month • Build time management habits • Set monthly OKRs • Do well in school • Stay active outside class • Build college knowledge
Fall	• Introduce yourself to counselor and teachers • Get familiar with high school graduation requirements • Find what makes you come alive: join 1–2 activities outside class • Update high school résumé (or you'll forget what you did)	
Early Spring	• Meet with counselor to discuss next year's courses; challenge yourself! • Deepen involvement in activities outside class • Learn about your school's available AP/IB courses • Start thinking about summer plans	
Late Spring	• Finalize 10th grade schedule; remember, colleges want to see rigor • Lock down summer plans by mid-May at latest • Update high school résumé (or you'll forget what you did)	

10th Grade: Step on It!		
	Time-Sensitive	**Ongoing**
Summer	• Stay busy: participate in a summer program you're passionate about • Read 2–3 books	• Read a book every month • Build time management habits • Set monthly OKRs • Do well in school • Stay active outside class • Build college knowledge
Early Fall	• Join an activity outside class; take on a leadership role if you're already involved in extracurriculars • Learn about and take the PSAT/NMSQT, if available	
Late Fall	• Review your PSAT/NMSQT scores; assess strengths and weaknesses • Attend a college fair if possible; record likes and dislikes • Update high school résumé (or you'll forget what you did)	
Early Spring	• Meet with counselor to discuss next year's courses; challenge yourself! • Deepen involvement in activities outside class • Get a Social Security number if you don't have one • Understand what, specifically, is tested on the ACT/SAT • February: Register for AP exams (if you're taking AP courses) • Start thinking about your summer plans	
Late Spring	• Finalize 11th grade schedule; remember, colleges want to see rigor • Early/mid-May: take AP exams (if you're taking AP courses) • Lock down summer plans by mid-May at latest • Update high school résumé (or you'll forget what you did)	

	11th Grade: This Just Got Real	
	Time-Sensitive	**Ongoing**
Summer	• Stay busy: participate in a summer program you're passionate about • Read 2–3 books	• Read a book every month • Build time management habits • Set monthly OKRs • Do well in school • Stay active outside class • Build college knowledge • Spend 3 hours on ACT/SAT prep weekly • Track ACT/ SAT registration deadlines
Early Fall	• Join an activity outside class; take on a leadership role if you're already involved in extracurriculars • Take the PSAT/NMSQT, if available • Decide when you will take the ACT/SAT; set reminders to register	
Late Fall	• Attend a college fair if possible; record likes and dislikes • Take a college tour if possible (can also be done in spring) • Review PSAT/NMSQT scores; assess strengths and weaknesses • Update high school résumé (or you'll forget what you did)	
Early Spring	• Meet with counselor to discuss next year's courses; challenge yourself! • Deepen involvement in activities outside class • Start thinking about possible mentors for college process • Start thinking about summer plans • Determine which, if any, SAT Subject Tests you will take • If English is your second language, decide when you'll take TOEFL • Start researching colleges to get a feel for what you want • Take a college tour, if possible	
Late Spring	• Finalize 12th grade schedule; remember, colleges want to see rigor • Lock down a college mentor; start seriously building college list • April: register for SAT Subject Tests (optional) • Early/mid-May: Take AP Exams (if you're taking AP courses) • Athletes: register with ncaa.org • Service academy prospects: start researching application process • Lock down summer plans by mid-May at the latest • Update high school résumé (or you'll forget what you did)	

Note: While the timeline below offers a solid overview, the timing of events in the college application process can vary hugely from student to student. Use this timeline as a guide, but pay close attention to the unique deadlines and requirements of each college you apply to and each scholarship you pursue.

	12th Grade: Game Time	
	Time-Sensitive	**Ongoing**
Summer	• Stay busy: participate in a summer program you're passionate about • Write strong drafts of 2–3 college essays • Use the time off from school to do major ACT/SAT prep	• Read a book every month • Build time management habits • Set monthly OKRs • Do well in school • Stay active outside class • Spend 2-3 hours on ACT/SAT prep weekly • Track ACT/SAT registration deadlines • Research and apply for scholarships • Track college and scholarship deadlines • Check your email multiple times a day
Aug/Sept	• Introduce yourself to and get on senior counselor's good side • Finalize college list; set up schedule of deadlines and requirements • Start scholarship list; set up schedule of deadlines and requirements • Decide when to apply to each of your colleges • Decide if/when you are going to take the ACT/SAT • Get help with writing activity description and college essays • Identify recommenders, and formally request recommendation letters • Request fee waivers, school report, official transcript from counselor	
Oct	• Oct 1: FAFSA opens; complete as close to Oct 1 as possible • Find and track your colleges' FAFSA and CSS PROFILE priority deadlines • Finalize activity description and all necessary essays • Polish high school résumé to include in college applications • Artists: finalize art portfolio to include in college applications • Follow up with recommenders; ensure they've submitted letters	
Nov	• Review applications with mentor; submit for Early and Rolling deadlines • Send official ACT/SAT, AP, and SAT Subject Test score reports to colleges	
Dec	• As admissions decisions arrive, read everything you receive carefully • Send thank-you letters to recommenders; notify them of admissions statuses • Prepare application components for Regular and remaining Rolling deadlines • Request fee waivers, school report, official transcript from counselor for remaining applications • Follow up with recommenders; ensure they've submitted letters for Regular and remaining Rolling deadlines	

Jan/Feb	• Finalize application components for remaining deadlines • February: register for AP exams (if you're taking AP courses) • Alert college financial aid offices of special family financial circumstances • Update your FAFSA with any additional colleges you've applied to since you filed it.
Mar/Apr	• Finalize application components for remaining deadlines • As admissions decisions arrive, read everything you receive carefully • Aggressively apply for outside scholarships • Weigh college and financial aid options • Choose a college and notify the others you won't be attending • Consider appealing financial aid award if necessary
May	• Early/mid-May: take AP exams (if you're taking AP courses) • Ask counselor to submit final transcript to college of choice • Register for fall courses, select housing and meal plans • Submit all required fees, medical forms, and other key documents • Make a personal budget for freshman fall semester

High School Courses Colleges Want to See

Different colleges have different <u>standards</u> and requirements for <u>admission</u>, but almost all want to see that you have taken certain high school courses. Below you will find the high school courses you need to have taken to be eligible to apply to four-year colleges. These are the <u>minimum</u>! Remember, colleges want to see that you have challenged yourself by taking the hardest courses you can handle.

English
Minimum/Recommended: 4 years, 8 credits

Take English all four years. The more seriously you approach reading and writing, the better you will perform on the ACT/SAT and in your college courses.

Math
Minimum: 3 years, 6 credits
Recommended: 4 years, 8 credits

Take a math course all four years. It's best if you increase the rigor each year. You can choose from the following courses, depending on your school and <u>proficiency</u> level:

- Geometry
- Pre-Algebra
- Algebra
- Algebra II
- Trigonometry
- Pre-Calculus
- Calculus

Science
Minimum: 3 years, 6 credits
Recommended: 4 years, 8 credits

Take at least three years of science. More selective colleges expect four years of science with lab work. At minimum, take the following:

- Biology
- Earth Science
- Chemistry or Physics

Social Studies
Minimum: 3 years, 6 credits
Recommended: 4 years, 8 credits

Take at least three years of social studies. More selective colleges like to see four. Your school may offer other social sciences, but here are some suggested courses:

- U.S. History
- U.S. Government
- World History
- Geography
- Psychology

Foreign Language
Minimum: 2 years, 4 credits
Recommended: 3–4 years, 6–8 credits

Find a foreign language that interests you and take more advanced courses as you progress through high school.

Arts
Minimum: 1 semester, 1 credit
Recommended: depends

Most colleges require at least one semester of visual or performing arts. Some colleges may ask for more, especially those with an arts focus. Follow your passions! If you love art, take an art course every year. Even if you don't care for art, know that it can stimulate your brain in ways other courses cannot.

Final notes

The list in this section shows what most colleges typically require. But there are two important things to know:

- Your high school may not require you to take as many courses or as many credit hours in order to graduate.

- Some colleges may require courses that are different from what your high school requires.

This is why it's important to stay in touch with both your high school counselor and your <u>prospective</u> colleges. In most high schools, one counselor supports hundreds of students, so you will need be <u>proactive</u> and communicate often to make sure you're on track to graduate. Colleges post on their websites the high school courses you need to have taken to qualify for admission. If you have your eye on a certain department or major, do some research (maybe even some emailing) to see if there are other, more rigorous classes they prefer you take in high school. This will set you up to have a competitive college application.

What You Need to Know About AP Courses

Advanced Placement (AP) courses are meant to give high school students a taste of college-level work. If you're on the fence about enrolling in one, I would usually say go for it, as long as you feel you can succeed by working hard. Some AP courses might be beyond your current ability level, no matter how hard you are willing to work - and that is okay. It's important to set ambitious but realistic goals.

Here are some reasons to take AP courses:

- **Better classes:** AP teachers are often the best teachers in school—not always but often. Having a great teacher can help you step up to the increased rigor.

- **Class Rank:** Colleges will evaluate your unweighted GPA (4.0 scale), so the GPA boost you get from AP courses doesn't matter all that much. However, a higher overall GPA could increase your class rank, which colleges do care about.

- **Course rigor:** You already know this! Colleges want to see that you've taken the hardest courses you can handle, and AP courses are at the top of that list.

- **College prep:** You don't just want to get into college; you want to do well while you're there. AP courses <u>mirror</u> the <u>pace</u>, workload, and rigor of intro college courses; <u>thus</u> they prepare you for the next level.

- **College credit:** Some, but not all, colleges award credit for qualifying AP exam scores (usually a 4 or 5). In this case, doing well on AP exams allows you to skip <u>repetitive</u> introductory courses and <u>fulfill</u> certain generation education requirements in the process. In short, you would get to take more classes you *want* to take rather than those you *have* to take.

- **Advanced course placement:** Instead of awarding credit for qualifying AP exam scores, some colleges will award advanced course placement, which lets you skip <u>repetitive</u> introductory courses. This lets you take more of the classes you want to take rather than those you have to take.

Attention: Colleges award credit and advanced course placement based on your AP exam scores, not your grades in your school's AP courses. What <u>constitutes</u> a "qualifying AP exam score" varies from school to school but can't be lower than a 3 out of 5.

How to figure out which AP courses are right for you

Each high school is different. It's up to you to find a person you trust who has the answers you seek. There may be more than one. Here are some suggestions...

- Ask your counselor if she/he feels you will succeed in the given course.

- If your school has one, ask your AP Coordinator if you should take the course.

- Ask peers or older students who have taken the course what they think.

- Talk to the teacher of the course; ask if she/he thinks you're ready for it.

- Read reviews about the course and its exam on The College Board's website.

What if you are home-schooled or your school doesn't offer AP courses?

AP courses are also offered online. Private course providers can be expensive, but others like the Florida Virtual School are state-sponsored. Do your research and ask around to find a course provider that works for you. If you are a homeschool student or attend a school that does not offer AP courses, I recommend you still take AP exams to demonstrate to colleges (and yourself) how you stack up nationally.

Lower Stress and Improve Results with Time Management

Time management is knowing what you have to do and when you will do it. My students, like most people, struggle with this. As a result, many of them:

- forget to turn in assignments,
- run out of time to prepare for quizzes and tests,
- constantly feel stressed, tired, and disorganized,
- don't always get the results they want.

Sound like you? It's okay. You can admit it.

If you follow the advice in this book, you will be busy: with schoolwork, extracurricular activities and, eventually, the college application process. If you don't manage your time effectively, you will quickly fall behind and feel <u>overwhelmed</u>.

Effective time management is not easy, but it is simple. People are not born effective time managers. They grow into them through a <u>steadfast</u> commitment to certain habits.

Below I have listed two sets of time management habits, a "beginner" level for <u>novices</u> and an "advanced" level for students with more experience.

Once again, time management isn't a talent. It's a skill set that people who are tired of being stressed and disorganized develop when they commit to taking the same smart steps over and over and over again.

Time Management Habits: Beginner Level

Sunday afternoon: enter each week with a clear view of what's coming.

- Think about your academic and non-academic responsibilities for the week ahead.
- Write in a notebook or planner what you have to get done and be ready for.
- Create a schedule for Monday, even if it will change.

Monday–Friday: enter each day with a schedule; write down all assignments.

- Adjust your daily schedule as needed; plan when you'll study and do homework.
- Throughout the day, write down all assignments and upcoming test/project dates.
- At night take a few minutes to set up the next day's schedule.

Time Management Habits: Advanced Level

Using the directions above as a foundation, <u>incorporate</u> these habits into your time management approach:

- Set weekly and daily schedules using an e-calendar; I recommend Google Calendar.
- For deadlines that are weeks or months out, create Google Calendar "events" and set email reminders so the due dates don't sneak up on you.
- Use your email inbox to stay organized: set your "unread" mail to appear at the top, and keep emails marked unread until you've read and taken care of the action steps inside them.
- If something comes up and you're on the go, email yourself about it; keep it marked as unread until you've dealt with it.

Use the "Time Management Tools" at the end of this chapter to put these habits into practice. You can also find it online at <u>www.masteryprep.com/cpb-resources</u>. The password is *CollegeSuccess*.

Stay on Track With Objectives and Key Results (OKRs)

We all have dreams we want to come true. A dream is like a road trip. The first step is deciding where you want to be at the end. You're reading this because you have a dream to attend a four-year college.

It would be nice if you could skip to the end but, like a long road trip, a dream must be broken into smaller, <u>manageable</u> checkpoints. These checkpoints keep you aimed at the final destination while reminding you that you are making <u>progress</u>.

If you want to stay on track to your dream of college, you must set short-term goals. They will keep you focused on what matters most and, each time you achieve one, you'll know you're *that* much closer to your vision.

I've never found a goal-setting <u>method</u> I like better than Objectives and Key Results, or "OKRs." This is a simple and effective way to stay focused and on track. Here's an example of an OKR:

Objective: Get in bathing-suit shape.

Key Result: Lose 15 pounds.

Habits:

1. Exercise for 45 minutes a day, 5 days a week.
2. Drink 64 ounces of water per day.
3. Eat no more than 2,000 calories per day.

An OKR is made up of three parts:

1. Objective—what you want to accomplish. It should be MAQS:

- **M**otivational: The way it's written, it's memorable and inspiring.
- **A**mbitious: Difficult, but possible, to achieve.
- **Q**ualitative: No numbers.
- **S**imple: Clear and straightforward.

2. Key Results—quantifiable indicators of success. They should be MARS:

•   **M**easurable: Must have a number.

•   **A**mbitious: Difficult, but possible, to achieve.

•   **R**esults-oriented: About outcomes, not actions.

•   **S**imple: Clear and straightforward.

3. Habits—actions you take regularly to achieve your Key Results.

Here's another example of an OKR:

Objective: Push my limits in APUSH (AP US History).

Key Results: End the semester with a 95%.

Habits:

1. Turn in my homework every day.
2. Read before class what we are going to cover in class that day.
3. Study for quizzes and tests with a reliable study partner.

Let's recap.

An Objective is a simple, memorable statement of what you want to achieve in a certain time period. I recommend setting OKRs for the month, but that is up to you.

Key Results are how you measure success. They must have numbers, or they are not Key Results. You can have up to 5 per Objective, but I suggest starting small with 1–2.

Habits are the smaller actions you will take consistently to achieve your Key Results.

The cool thing about OKRs is they are useful in all areas of life, whether you are trying to get fitter, do better in a class, learn an instrument, and beyond.

As I said, you can set OKRs for any time period, but I recommend a monthly rhythm. Here's what yours could look like:

End of the month: Set OKRs for the upcoming month.

Daily: Track completion of Habits.

Sundays: Assess if you've made progress toward your Key Results. What changes, if any, should you make to your habits?

End of the month:

1. Assess if you achieved your Key Results.
2. Reflect: What lessons did you learn from this process? What adjustments do you need to make to next month's OKRs?
3. Set OKRs for the upcoming month.

For each month, you should have no more than 3 Objectives, and each Objective should have no more than 5 Key Results. When you first start out, limit your Key Results to 1–2 per Objective. Setting your OKRs doesn't mean you ignore everything else in your life. It just means these are the things you've chosen to focus on this month. These are the things that will move you toward your dream. You may find it hard to decide what your OKRs are, and that's okay! It's part of the learning process.

Last thing: you *must* record your OKRs, whether on paper or typed up. If you don't, I promise things won't work out the way you want.

I hope you put this to use and find it helpful! At BRYC, we use OKRs with students. The ones who have taken them seriously have seen amazing results.

Find What Makes You Come Alive

"Don't ask what the world needs. Ask what makes you come alive and go do it. Because what the world needs is people who have come alive." –Howard Thurman

When you discover what you love spending hours and hours doing, you engage in a kind of learning that can't happen in a classroom. You learn how to work with others, lead, solve real problems, give and receive tough <u>feedback</u>, and more. Above all, you learn who you are—what makes you come alive.

Colleges, particularly the more selective ones, are looking for students who have come alive through their commitments outside the classroom. College admissions officers are trying to build diverse campus communities, and they know that what you bring to the table goes far beyond your GPA and ACT/SAT scores.

Here are answers to frequently asked questions about extracurricular involvement.

What are colleges specifically looking for?

Colleges want to see deep involvement in 1-3 extracurricular activities throughout your high school career. It's best if your involvement increases over time. By the time you graduate, you might have participated in 10 activities, but you can only give your heart to a few. There isn't time for much more.

Do I have to be president of the club or captain of the team?

If you hold leadership roles, you <u>distinguish</u> yourself from other applicants. But your involvement isn't <u>discounted</u> if you don't have a leadership role.

Are some activities more impressive than others?

No. Do what makes you come alive. If you don't love it, you shouldn't be doing it. Whatever you do, go hard at it.

When should I start getting involved?

Start right away. Take time during your freshman year to explore which activities your school offers. You don't have to be 100% sold on any of them. If you're interested in an activity, give it a shot and see where it takes you. It can help to join with a friend.

Is it ever too late to get involved?

No. It's great to find what you love freshman year and do it throughout high school, but most students aren't so lucky. Keep searching until you find your thing, and then go for it. One <u>caveat</u>: I generally don't recommend picking up a new activity senior year. By then you have one foot out the door, and colleges won't be <u>overly</u> impressed with a one-year commitment. But hey, if you love something, go for it!

Does it count as involvement if it's not an activity my school offers?

Absolutely. Involvement is involvement. That includes jobs, internships, commitments at your place of worship, an organization you started, volunteering in the community, and more.

What if I can't get involved because I need to be home helping out?

Colleges are starting to realize that many teenagers play vital roles at home—cooking, cleaning, caring for siblings—and they recognize these family responsibilities as an important type of involvement.

What if I don't know what makes me "come alive?"

Then you are not alone. Search your soul. Speak to people who know and love you. But also know the best way to figure out what you do and don't love is to take a risk and try something. If you get it wrong, you will have learned something important about yourself.

Does it matter what I do over the summer?

Yes, for two reasons. First, if you just chill over the summer, you will <u>regress</u> academically. Truth: you will get dumber. Second, colleges want to see that you were productive during the summer. Sports, clubs, service projects, jobs—it all counts. It's great if you can do the same thing every summer, but it's not a must.

Discovering what makes you come alive is a lifelong process. You probably won't get it right the first time, but you won't get it right ever if you just stand on the sidelines. Take smart risks. Explore. Sometimes you hit the jackpot; other times you cut your losses and quit. In either case, you learn about yourself and grow.

How to Craft a Solid Résumé

Involvement is one of the "Big Five" that colleges <u>evaluate</u>. This <u>refers</u> to your engagement outside of class in sports, clubs, work, summer programs, etc. When it's time to apply to college, you'll want to describe your participation in these activities. How effectively you do that will impact your admissions chances (see "How to Write a Great Activity Description" in chapter 5 for more).

By the time students get to senior year, many have forgotten all the amazing things they did throughout high school. That's why I urge students to update their résumés after every semester, starting in 9th grade. Those who do have a much easier time describing their activities on college applications. There are other benefits, too:

- Colleges now allow applicants to upload résumés in addition to their activity descriptions. I recommend this as a way to show off another skill.

- By maintaining a résumé, you will keep a record of your awards and honors, which most colleges also ask for.

- By maintaining a résumé, you will be ready at a moment's notice to apply for jobs or internships.

- Recommenders appreciate having students' updated résumés. It makes writing recommendation letters much easier.

Not all résumés need to look the same but, as you will see in this section, I recommend a very simple structure:

- Personal information goes at the top: name, address, phone number, email
- Education: expected graduation date (month and year), GPA, ACT/SAT composite score, class rank (if applicable), intended major, career aspiration
- In-school extracurricular commitments
- Outside-of-school extracurricular commitments
- Employment experience and personal responsibilities
- Honors and awards
- About me: personal interests and qualities

When you're describing your outside-of-school extracurricular commitments, there are two important things to keep in mind:

1. **Include the most impressive info:** Use your limited space to very specifically describe your responsibilities, <u>contributions</u>, <u>promotions</u>, and achievements. If you had to apply or try out for the activity, make sure to point that out.

2. **If it's not clear, say it:** If the activity isn't self-explanatory, provide a very brief explanation so the reader knows what you're talking about. You will see an examples in the sample résumé in this section.

Below are eleven tips for crafting a solid résumé. I'll call these out as they appear on the next page.

Eleven Résumé Tips:

1. **Template:** Make life easy by putting your information into a pre-made Microsoft Word template, available through Word or downloaded off the web.

2. **Length:** As you update your résumé throughout high school, it doesn't matter how long it gets. But the final, <u>polished</u> version that you submit to colleges or recommenders should be no longer than one page.

3. **Font:** Pick a font type that is simple, mature, and professional.

4. **Color:** It's okay to show some personality by using small doses of color; just make sure it doesn't look like a clown's résumé, and keep the main text black or dark grey.

5. **Alignment:** Your résumé needs to look clean and neat; make sure all bullet points line up perfectly.

6. **Strong, specific verbs:** Use strong verbs to describe specifically what you have done in your various activities.

7. **Grammatical consistency:** Usual grammar rules don't apply. Fragments are fine, as long as you use them consistently.

8. **Punctuation consistency:** Usual punctuation rules don't apply. Just make sure to punctuate consistently throughout your résumé.

9. **Formatting consistency:** The physical setup of each bullet point of information should be consistent throughout your résumé and especially within each section.

10. **Tense:** Use past tense for verbs if the action is no longer happening, present tense for verbs if the action is still happening.

11. **Chronological order:** List your activities in chronological order, starting with the most recent ones and working your way backward.

Music Résumé:

Whether they sing, play instruments, or both, musicians should also submit music résumés with their college applications so they can share their experiences, qualifications, and accomplishments within this specific realm. See the example on page 44.

Résumé Example

Here is an example of an excellent student résumé. Read the comments on the next page to see what this student did well.

GARRINECIA SINGLETON

1234 College Drive · Baton Rouge, Louisiana 70802 · (555)-555-5555 · garrinecia@gmail.com

---

EDUCATION

SCOTLANDVILLE MAGNET HIGH SCHOOL, ENGINEERING PROGRAM, EXPECTED GRADUATION: MAY 2018
- GPA (unweighted): 3.8
- ACT composite: 23
- Class rank: 2/250
- Intended major: Psychology
- Career aspiration: Psychologist

IN-SCHOOL EXTRACURRICULAR COMMITMENTS

- **NATIONAL HONOR SOCIETY, MEMBER (AUG 2017-PRESENT):** Participants recognized for outstanding academics, handpicked by teachers; mentor students at Ryan Elementary School, assisting with homework and personal issues and conducting annual gift drive.
- **STUDENT LEADERSHIP COUNCIL, AMBASSADOR (AUG 2017-PRESENT):** Recruit middle school students; welcome and orient new students and their families; represent school and speak at important internal and external events.
- **TEAM SPIRIT, SECRETARY (AUG 2016-PRESENT):** Club raises awareness around drug- and alcohol-related issues at Scotlandville and local elementary and middle schools; as Secretary, take meeting minutes and manage operations and finances at all events.
- **NASA ROVER CHALLENGE, CHAIRPERSON (AUG 2014-MAY 2016):** Club collaborates with Jacobs engineers to design a "moon buggy" that will race at competition in Huntsville, AL; as Chair, conducted meetings and assigned all roles; club was discontinued in May 2016.

IN-SCHOOL EXTRACURRICULAR COMMITMENTS

- **BATON ROUGE YOUTH LEADERSHIP COUNCIL, CHAIRPERSON (AUG 2017-PRESENT):** Handpicked to join youth advisory group that collaborates with Mayor in identifying and solving major community problems; as Chair, lead all meetings and planning and execution of events.
- **YOUTH VOLUNTEER CORPS, CORPS MEMBER (AUG 2014-MAY 2017):** With Capital Area United Way, participated in monthly community service projects across the city, ranging from assisting senior citizens to supervising children during a summer camp.

EMPLOYMENT EXPERIENCE & PERSONAL RESPONSIBILITIES

- **ZAXBY'S, LEAD CASHIER (FEB 2017-PRESENT):** Manage all cash register duties; oversee colleagues to ensure transactions are carried out precisely and efficiently; maintain orderliness and cleanliness of lobby; deliver best-in-class customer service.
- **CARETAKER (2012-PRESENT):** Support younger brother with all tasks imaginable: transport him to after-school and weekend activities; ensure he completes his homework; buy groceries and cook for him; and look after him when my mother is unable to.

HONORS

- Academic: A/B Honor Roll (2015-2016); Dean's List (2015-2016); Student of the Year Runner-Up (2017- 2018); Salutatorian (Present)

ABOUT ME

- **Skills:** Verbal and written communication, time management, organization, MS Office proficiency
- **Qualities:** Confident, resilient, reliable, assertive, trustworthy, practical, dedicated, hardworking

GARRINECIA SINGLETON

1234 College Drive · Baton Rouge, Louisiana 70802 · (555)-555-5555 · garrinecia@gmail.com

EDUCATION

SCOTLANDVILLE MAGNET HIGH SCHOOL, ENGINEERING PROGRAM, EXPECTED GRADUATION: MAY 2018
- GPA (unweighted): 3.8
- ACT composite: 23
- Class rank: 2/250
- Intended major: Psychology
- Career aspiration: Psychologist

IN-SCHOOL EXTRACURRICULAR COMMITMENTS

- **NATIONAL HONOR SOCIETY, MEMBER (AUG 2017-PRESENT):** Participants recognized for outstanding academics, handpicked by teachers; mentor students at Ryan Elementary School, assisting with homework and personal issues and conducting annual gift drive.
- **STUDENT LEADERSHIP COUNCIL, AMBASSADOR (AUG 2017-PRESENT):** Recruit middle school students; welcome and orient new students and their families; represent school and speak at important internal and external events.
- **TEAM SPIRIT, SECRETARY (AUG 2016-PRESENT):** Club raises awareness around drug- and alcohol-related issues at Scotlandville and local elementary and middle schools; as Secretary, take meeting minutes and manage operations and finances at all events.
- **NASA ROVER CHALLENGE, CHAIRPERSON (AUG 2014-MAY 2016):** Club collaborates with Jacobs engineers to design a "moon buggy" that will race at competition in Huntsville, AL; as Chair, conducted meetings and assigned all roles; club was discontinued in May 2016.

IN-SCHOOL EXTRACURRICULAR COMMITMENTS

- **BATON ROUGE YOUTH LEADERSHIP COUNCIL, CHAIRPERSON (AUG 2017-PRESENT):** Handpicked to join youth advisory group that collaborates with Mayor in identifying and solving major community problems; as Chair, lead all meetings and planning and execution of events.
- **YOUTH VOLUNTEER CORPS, CORPS MEMBER (AUG 2014-MAY 2017):** With Capital Area United Way, participated in monthly community service projects across the city, ranging from assisting senior citizens to supervising children during a summer camp.

EMPLOYMENT EXPERIENCE & PERSONAL RESPONSIBILITIES

- **ZAXBY'S, LEAD CASHIER (FEB 2017-PRESENT):** Manage all cash register duties; oversee colleagues to ensure transactions are carried out precisely and efficiently; maintain orderliness and cleanliness of lobby; deliver best-in-class customer service.
- **CARETAKER (2012-PRESENT):** Support younger brother with all tasks imaginable: transport him to after-school and weekend activities; ensure he completes his homework; buy groceries and cook for him; and look after him when my mother is unable to.

HONORS

- Academic: A/B Honor Roll (2015-2016); Dean's List (2015-2016); Student of the Year Runner-Up (2017- 2018); Salutatorian (Present)

ABOUT ME

- **Skills:** Verbal and written communication, time management, organization, MS Office proficiency
- **Qualities:** Confident, resilient, reliable, assertive, trustworthy, practical, dedicated, hardworking

---

Résumé Tip #1 — Template: This template was pulled straight from MS Word. Made it so much easier. Just put the information in.

Résumé Tip #2 — Length: A polished résumé should not exceed one page, and this is no exception!

Résumé Tip #3 — Font type: The font is Calibri. It's simple, clean, and professional-looking.

Résumé Tip #4 — Color: This is printed in black and white, but the original résumé put the these headings in a dark-green font. This makes the résumé a bit more visually interesting, while not being not over the top.

Résumé Tip #5 — Alignment: The alignment is perfection! I dare you to try and find one bullet or sentence that's out of place. You can't!

Résumé Tip #6 — Use action verbs! Recruit students. Welcome and orient new students. Represent school.

Résumé Tip #7 — Grammatical consistency: In the three largest sections, the writer uses fragments consistently throughout. All fragments begin with action verbs, except in cases like this one, where she begins by briefly explaining what the activity is.

Résumé Tip #10 — Tense: Notice here she switches to past tense since she is no longer conducting meetings as chairperson since May 2016.

Résumé Tip #9 — Formatting consistency: Within every section, and especially in the three largest, each bullet point of information is physically set up the same way. First she lists the activity name, then there's a comma, then her position, and then in parentheses the timing of her participation. These are in caps and bolded. Every activity description looks identical, and the consistency is the same within the other sections.

Résumé Tip #6 — Use action verbs! Manage cash register. Oversee colleagues. Maintain orderliness. Deliver customer service.

Résumé Tip #8 — Punctuation consistency: Within every section, commas and semicolons are used consistently. In the three largest sections, commas always separate the activity name and her position within it, and semicolons separate the things she did in the given activity.

Music Résumé Example

Ja'Colby Jermaine Freeman – Music Résumé

1234 College Drive | Baton Rouge, Louisiana 70802 | (555) 555-5555 | jacolby@gmail.com

Objective

I seek a rich and rigorous music education program through which I can continue to foster my passions while preparing for my ultimate goal: healing others through music.

Education

HIGH SCHOOL DIPLOMA | EXP: MAY 2019 | MCKINLEY SENIOR HIGH SCHOOL – BATON ROUGE, LOUISIANA
- GPA (weighted cumulative): 4.14
- ACT: 26 (composite); 29 (super score)
- Class Rank: 11/291

Musical Career

VOCAL
- A Capella Choir (2016-2019) – First and Second Tenor
- Talented Music (2010-2015) – Vocalist
- Gospel Choir (2015-2016) – Tenor
- Advanced Choir (2015) – Tenor and Alto
- Intermediate Choir (2014) – Tenor
- Beginning Choir (2013) – Alto

INSTRUMENTAL
- Marching Band (2015-2019) – Trombone, Baritone, F Horn, Clarinet
- Intermediate Orchestra (2018-2019) – Clarinet, 1st and 2nd Chair; Baritone, 1st Chair
- Jazz Band (2017-2018) – Trombone, 1st Chair
- Intermediate Band (2015-2016) – Trombone
- Concert Band (2013-2014) – Trombone, Clarinet
- Intermediate Choir (2014) – Tenor
- Elementary Concert Band (2010) – Saxophone

Awards and Honors

- Section Leader, Lower Brass (2018-2019)
- Most Dedicated, Marching Band (2017-2018)
- Co-Section Leader, Baritone (2017-2018)
- Outstanding Musical Achievement and Performance, Gospel Choir (2015-2016)
- Most Improved Freshman Male, Marching Band (2015-2016)

Time Management Tools

Habit 1A - Plan

Before a new week begins, take time on Sunday to think about what you will have to accomplish in the week ahead. Think about your academic and non-academic responsibilities. Here are two questions to get you thinking:

- Do I have any big assessments (i.e. quizzes and tests) due or deadlines coming up?
- Do I have any appointments, meetings, or other events coming up, and do I need to do anything to prepare for them?

Week of:						
Academic						
Class 1	**Class 2**	**Class 3**	**Class 4**	**Class 5**	**Class 6**	**Class 7**

Non-Academic				
College Process/ Activity 1	**Job**	**Activity 2**	**Activity 3**	**Personal**

Habit 1B - Plan

Calendar things you know are happening in the week ahead: school, after-school programs, work hours, practices, appointments, meetings, and anything else you know is coming up. Also, block off "flexible time," which is time when you can complete homework, etc.

Weekly Schedule - Week of:							
	M	**T**	**W**	**TH**	**F**	**SAT**	**SUN**
7:00 AM							
8:00 AM							
9:00 AM							
10:00 AM							
11:00 AM							
12:00 PM							
1:00 PM							
2:00 PM							
3:00 PM							
4:00 PM							
5:00 PM							
6:00 PM							
7:00 PM							
8:00 PM							
9:00 PM							
10:00 PM							
11:00 PM							
12:00 AM							

Habit 2 - Monitor

Throughout the week, track everything you have to do as soon as you learn about it. Don't delay. As soon as you learn about an assignment or upcoming test, quiz, or project, write it down right away. In other words, monitor what you have to do throughout the week.

Assignment & Assessment Tracker - Week of:						
	M	**T**	**W**	**TH**	**F**	**SAT/SUN**
Class 1						
Class 2						
Class 3						
Class 4						
Class 5						
Class 6						
Class 7						
Activities						

Habit 3 - Assess

After school, look at your assignment tracker and your weekly schedule. Take stock of everything you have to get done and when you will get it done. Update your weekly schedule to reflect this plan. Don't forget to include time for eating, sleeping, showering, etc.

Habit 4 - Break

Take care of yourself. Sleep. Exercise. Eat well enough. Do things that bring you joy. Prepare mentally to begin the cycle again.

In Summary...

- College want to see the Big Five: 1) high grades in tough courses; 2) solid ACT or SAT scores; 3) powerful essays; 4) deep involvement outside of class; and 5) strong recommendation letters from teachers and mentors.

- Make sure you know which courses you need to have taken to graduate high school as well as which courses you need to have taken to be competitive for colleges you want to apply to.

- When you are ready to take and succeed in AP courses, they will lead to many benefits.

- It is important during the college application process to remain organized, manage your time effectively, and set ambitious, realistic goals.

- Find 1–3 non-academic activities you love, and get deeply involved with them.

- For many reasons, it's wise to maintain a sharp, well-crafted résumé.

Doing Well on Tests

What You Need to Know About the PSAT/NMSQT

What's the PSAT/NMSQT?

Also known as the National Merit Scholarship Qualifying Test (NMSQT), the Preliminary SAT (PSAT) is a standardized test that high school students take to get a sense of how they'll do on the SAT or ACT and to determine if they qualify for a National Merit Scholarship. There are two main sections: 1) Evidenced-Based Reading and Writing and 2) Math.

Who takes the PSAT/NMSQT?

High school sophomores and juniors usually take the PSAT/NMSQT, but younger students are eligible to take the test if they choose.

Why take the PSAT/NMSQT?

- It can give you an early <u>indication</u> of your SAT or ACT score
- You can use the results to <u>identify</u> weak spots when prepping for the SAT
- Students who take the PSAT score higher on the SAT on average
- If you score well, you can qualify for the National Merit scholarship

Do colleges require that I take the PSAT/NMSQT?

Colleges do not require you to take the PSAT/NMSQT because it is not a college entrance exam. This test will have almost no impact on your college application process unless you qualify for the National Merit Scholarship process.

If I do badly on the PSAT/NMQST, will it hurt me in the college application process?

Nope. Taking the PSAT/NMSQT can only help you. You get to practice taking a long, standardized test, and you can <u>analyze</u> your results to figure out what you need to improve for the SAT or ACT.

How long is the PSAT/NMSQT?

2 hours and 45 minutes.

When is the PSAT/NMSQT offered?

The PSAT/NMSQT is offered in the fall, usually in October or November.

How is the PSAT/NMQST scored?

Each correct response is worth one point, and no points are deducted for missing a question. Your total score, which is the sum of the two main sections, will range from a minimum of 320 to a maximum of 1520.

How much does it cost to take an PSAT/NMQST?

It costs $16 to register. Some high schools cover student fees, while other high school charge students to take it. Fee waivers are available for lower-income 11th-graders. Schools, not students, request fee waivers.

How do you prepare for the PSAT/NMQST?

- **Get a prep book:** These are for sale at local bookstores or online, but they're expensive. Alternate options: buy it used, check it out of a public library, or borrow it from a friend who doesn't need it anymore.

- **Search online:** There are tons of free online resources to help you prepare for the PSAT/NMQST. Just one example is Kahn Academy.

- **Talk to people who've been there:** Talk to seniors at your high school. They will have taken the test before and can give you some advice.

- **Study with others:** Talking through material with others is an effective learning strategy and generally more fun than reading alone.

How do you register for the PSAT/NMSQT?

You will register for the PSAT/NMQST through your high school. If your school doesn't offer it, speak to your counselor about registering independently.

For more info, visit collegereadiness.collegeboard.org/psat-nmsqt-psat-10.

What You Need to Know About the SAT

What's the SAT?

It's a standardized college entrance exam designed to measure your readiness for college-level classes. It measures you on math, reading, and writing.

Who takes the SAT?

Students of all ages can take the SAT, but high school juniors and seniors primarily take this test as they are getting ready to apply to college.

Why take the SAT?

- Most colleges require that you submit an SAT (or ACT) score.
- Even for colleges that don't require it, a high SAT score will set you apart.
- A high SAT score will make you more competitive for scholarships.
- In some cases, a high SAT score allows you to earn college credit.

Do colleges require that I take the SAT?

Most four-year colleges will want to see either an SAT or ACT score as part of your application. In a few pages, you will read that some colleges are flexible on this. Even at those colleges, a high SAT score will make you a more competitive applicant.

Can I take the SAT multiple times, and if so, will colleges see all my attempts?

You can take the SAT pretty much as many times as you want, and most colleges won't make you report all your scores. It's very common for students to take the SAT multiple times.

How long is the SAT?

Long. It's between 3 and 4 hours, depending on if you take the essay section, which is optional.

When is the SAT offered?

The College Board offers the SAT seven times a year at thousands of testing sites across the nation. Some high schools offer the SAT and administer it during the regular school day.

How is the SAT scored?

Each correct response is worth one point. No points are deducted for a missing question. The score on the SAT ranges from a minimum of 400 to a maximum of 1600.

How much does it cost to take an SAT?

It costs $47.50 to register for the SAT and $64.50 if you take the essay section. If your high school administers the test, you likely won't have to pay a fee. Lower-income 11th- and 12th-graders may qualify for a fee waiver. Learn more about fee waivers at collegereadiness. collegeboard.org/sat/register/fees/fee-waivers.

How do you prepare for the SAT?

- **Get a prep book:** These are for sale at local bookstores or online, but they're expensive. Alternate options: buy it used, check it out of a public library, or borrow it from a friend who doesn't need it anymore.

- **Search online:** There are tons of free online resources to help you prepare for the SAT. Just one example is Kahn Academy.

- **Talk to people who've been there:** Talk to seniors at your high school. They will have taken the test before and can give you some advice.

- **Study with others:** Talking through material with others is an effective learning strategy and generally more fun than reading alone.

How do you register for the SAT?

Register online at an official testing site near you by by following the info here: collegereadiness.collegeboard.org/sat/register/online-registration-help.

If you take the test through your school, your school will help you register.

For more info, visit collegereadiness.collegeboard.org/sat.

What You Need to Know About the ACT

What's the ACT?

It is (the other) standardized college entrance exam designed to measure your <u>readiness</u> for college-level classes. It measures you on English, math, reading, and science.

Who takes the ACT?

Students of all ages can take the ACT, but high school juniors and seniors primarily take this test as they are getting ready to apply to college.

Why take the ACT?

- Most colleges require that you submit an ACT (or SAT) score.
- Even for colleges that don't require it, a high ACT score will set you apart.
- A high ACT score will make you more competitive for scholarships.
- In some cases, a high ACT score allows you to earn college credit.

Do colleges require that I take the ACT?

Most four-year colleges will want to see either an ACT or SAT score as part of your application. In a few pages, you will read that some colleges are flexible on this. Even at those colleges, a high ACT score will make you a more competitive applicant.

Can I take the ACT multiple times and, if so, will colleges see all my <u>attempts</u>?

You can take the ACT pretty much as many times as you want, and most colleges won't make you report all your scores. It's very common for students to take the ACT multiple times.

How long is the ACT?

Long. It's between 3 and 4 hours, depending on if you take the writing section, which is optional.

When is the ACT offered?

The ACT is offered seven times a year at thousands of testing sites across the nation. Some high schools offer the ACT and <u>administer</u> it during the regular school day.

How is the ACT scored?

Each correct response is worth one point. No points are deducted for missing a question. Each subsection—English, math, reading, science—is scored from 1 to 36. Your <u>composite</u> score will be the average of those four subscores.

How much does it cost to take an ACT?

It costs $46 to register for the ACT and $62.50 if you take the optional writing section. f your high school administers the test, you likely won't have to pay a fee. Lower-income 11th- and 12th-graders may qualify for a fee waiver. You'll need to speak to your counselor about securing such a waiver.

How do you prepare for the ACT?

- **Get a prep book:** These are for sale at local bookstores or online, but they're expensive. Alternate options: buy it used, check it out of a public library, or borrow it from a friend who doesn't need it anymore.

- **Search online:** There are tons of free online resources to help you prepare for the ACT. Just one example is Kahn Academy.

- **Talk to people who've been there:** Talk to seniors at your high school. They will have taken the test before and can give you some advice.

- **Study with others:** Talking through material with others is an effective learning strategy and generally more fun than reading alone.

How do you register for the ACT?

Register online at <u>www.act.org</u>. This is also your hub for general information about the ACT. If you take the test through your school, your school will help you register.

What You Need to Know About the TOEFL

What's the TOEFL?

The Test of English as a Foreign Language is a standardized test designed to measure the English language ability of students who do not speak English as a first language and wish to enroll in English-speaking colleges. The test measures a student's ability to read, verbally <u>comprehend</u>, speak, and write English.

Who takes the TOEFL?

For the most part, high school juniors and seniors who do not speak English as their first language and want to attend English-speaking colleges take the TOEFL.

Why take the TOEFL?

- The TOEFL is generally required if you do not speak English as your primary language.
- You can use your TOEFL score to qualify for certain scholarships.
- The TOEFL can help you determine how ready you are to enter college in an English-speaking country.

Do colleges require that I take the TOEFL?

By default, colleges do not require students to take the TOEFL. You may, however, be asked to take the TOEFL if you have not been using English as your primary language in the past 5 years. Every college and university will differ somewhat, so be sure to check their requirements.

If I do badly on the TOEFL, will it hurt me in the college application process?

The short answer is yes. If you do poorly on your TOEFL, you may not be accepted to your program. Every college is different, so check their minimum requirements. If you score below the requirement, you will need to retake the test. There is no benefit for scoring above the requirement, so set your study plan based on the minimum number necessary.

How long is the TOEFL?

Between 3 and 4.5 hours, depending on the length of the Reading and Listening sections on the test.

When is the TOEFL offered?

The TOEFL is offered multiple times a year. Check www.ets.org/bin/getprogram.cgi?test=toefl for availability.

How is the TOEFL scored?

Each question answered correctly are worth 1 to 3 points. There is no penalty for missing questions, so make sure to answer every question. The TOEFL is scored on a scale of 0 to 120.

How much does it cost to take the TOEFL?

It costs $205 to register for the TOEFL. You may qualify for a fee waiver, so check with your counselor.

How do you prepare for the TOEFL?

- **Get a TOEFL book:** You can buy these at a local bookstore or online, but they're expensive. Alternate options: buy them used, check them out of a public library, or borrow them from a friend who doesn't need them anymore.

- **Search online:** ETS offers a free course that you can use: www.edx.org/course/toeflr-test-preparation-insiders-guide-etsx-toeflx-4.

- **Talk to people who've been there:** Talk to other students at your high school. If you don't know anyone who has taken the test, ask your counselor for advice.

- **Study with others:** Talking through material with others is a more effective learning strategy than reading alone. It's also more fun.

How do you register for the TOEFL?

You can register online by following the information at this link: v2.ereg.ets.org/ereg/public/route?_p=TEL.

How do I get more info?

Go to https://www.ets.org/toefl.

The ACT/SAT Can Be Optional

You might feel a cool wave of relief wash over you upon learning that lots of four-year colleges are de-emphasizing the ACT and SAT in the college admissions process. In fact more than 1,000 four-year colleges now consider themselves "test optional" or "test flexible."

Test optional means you can apply without submitting an ACT/SAT score at all, and *test flexible* means a student can submit AP and/or SAT Subject test scores instead. Visit www.fairtest.org to see the full list of schools that are test optional, test flexible, or that weigh test scores less heavily in the admissions process.

These schools are part of a growing movement recognizing that standardized testing is an unfair barrier to college for underrepresented students and those who can't afford expensive test prep courses and materials. Test-optional and test-flexible colleges have found that students who do not submit ACT and SAT scores can perform just as well academically in collegeas their peers who do submit them.

None of this means test-optional and test-flexible schools are easier to get into; their admissions requirements are just different. With ACT and SAT scores out of the equation, your grades, essays, recommendation letters, extracurriculars, and interviews would take up more of the spotlight. Many test-optional and text-flexible colleges also require supplemental materials, like a research paper, a portfolio of your best high school work, or some other alternative assignment. As always you must pay attention to each college's unique requirements.

Still, I discourage you from torching your ACT/SAT prep books in a celebratory bonfire. My aim is to let you know there are options. You should hustle to grow your ACT/SAT score; if you're reading this book, there's a good chance you have the resources to do so. Strong ACT or SAT scores will differentiate you positively, and you should submit them if they will strengthen your application.

How do you know if they will strengthen your application? If you're looking at a test-optional or test-flexible school and debating submitting your scores, the rule of thumb is to see how your scores compare to the school's average for incoming freshmen. If your scores are within or above the middle 50-percent range, send them in!

What You Need to Know About AP Exams

What's an AP exam?

It's the final exam a student takes after a year-long AP course. All AP exams include both a multiple-choice and free-response section. The exception is AP Studio Art, which only requires students to submit a portfolio.

Who takes AP exams?

Usually students take an AP exam after they've taken an AP course in high school, but you don't have to have taken an AP course to take the end-of-year exam. You also don't have to take an AP exam just because you've taken the course. The simplest answer is: anyone can take an AP exam.

Why should I take an AP exam?

- At some high schools, AP exams count as final grades for AP courses.

- Depending on the college, a qualifying AP exam score (no lower than 3) can earn you college credit, enabling you to skip introductory college courses.

- Strong AP exam scores will strengthen your college application.

- AP exams give you a glimpse of college-level exams.

- AP course rigor varies by high school, but AP exams are the same for all students. Scoring well on them shows you are nationally competitive.

If I do badly on AP exams, will it hurt me in the college application process?

No. It's your choice whether or not to report your AP exam scores.

How long does an AP exam take?

Usually 2-3 hours.

When are AP exams offered?

May of each year.

How is the multiple-choice section scored?

For every correct response, you get a point. For every incorrect response, ¼ of a point is deducted. You are neither rewarded nor penalized for skipping questions.

How much does it cost to take an AP exam?

About $90, but there are ways to get AP testing fees reduced or eliminated. To learn more, visit www.collegeboard.org/testing.

How do you prepare for an AP exam?

*   **Get an AP review book:** You can buy these at a local bookstore or online, but they're expensive. Alternate options: buy them used, check them out of a public library, or borrow them from a friend who doesn't need them anymore.

*   **Search online:** There are tons of helpful, free online resources to prepare for AP exams.

*   **Talk to people who've been there:** Students who have already taken the same exam(s) might have helpful advice for you.

*   **Study with others:** Talking through material with others is a more effective learning strategy than reading alone. It's also more fun.

How do I register for an AP exam?

Your AP coordinator or high school counselor should assist you with the AP exam registration process. If you are homeschooled or your school doesn't offer AP exams, you can visit apstudent.collegeboard. org/takingtheexam/registering-for-exams.

How do I get more info?

For more information about AP exams, including upcoming exam dates, accommodations for students with special needs, what to bring on test day, and more, go to apstudent.collegeboard.org/home. If you don't already have an account, you will need to create one (for free) with College Board.

What You Need to Know About SAT Subject Tests

What's an SAT Subject Test?

Also called "SAT II," SAT Subjects Tests are standardized tests in specific subjects like Math, Biology, History, etc.

Why take SAT Subject Tests?

- Some colleges require them.
- Some colleges strongly recommend them.
- Unlike SAT/ACT, you can choose to test in your strongest subjects.
- Strong SAT II scores distinguish you from other applicants.
- They give you a glimpse of college-level exams.
- They show how you stack up with students across the nation.
- Strong SAT II scores can earn you college credit or the opportunity to skip intro-level college courses, depending on the college.
- Students whose first language is not English can use SAT II to show strength in subjects that don't heavily <u>emphasize</u> English skills.

Do colleges require that I take SAT Subject Tests?

It depends on the college, but most don't. Pay attention to each school's requirements, especially if you are applying to a specific program at that college. In general, taking SAT Subject Tests is a way to go the extra mile to distinguish yourself from other applicants. Remember, too, that some test-flexible schools permit you to submit SAT Subject Test scores in place of ACT or SAT scores.

Which SAT Subject Tests can I take?

There are 20 tests spanning five subjects: English, History, Languages, Math, and Science. For a list of all available tests, go to sat.collegeboard.org/register.

If I do poorly on SAT Subject Tests, will it hurt me in the application process?

No. It's your choice whether or not to report your SAT Subject Test scores.

How long do they take?

Each exam lasts one hour.

When are SAT Subject Tests offered?

They are offered six times a year on the same dates the SAT is offered (except in March). These dates change every year, so Google it!

How are the tests scored?

For every correct response, you get one point. For every incorrect response, a fraction of a point is deducted. You are neither rewarded nor penalized for questions you skip.

How much does it cost to take an SAT Subject Test?

Each SAT Subject Test costs $22. In addition, the registration fee costs $26 per test date. If you're taking multiple SAT Subject Tests, it makes financial sense to knock them out in one day. Eligible students may be able to receive a fee waiver from College Board, high school counselors, and certain community-based organizations. Find out if you are eligible for a fee waiver at collegereadiness.collegeboard. org/sat-subject-tests/register/fees-payments/fee-waivers.

How do I register for an SAT Subject Test?

Go to sat.collegeboard.org/register/sat-subject-test-dates. If you don't already have an account, you will need to create one (for free) with College Board.

How do I get more info?

Go to sat.collegeboard.org/about-tests/sat-subject-tests. The College Board provides all the information you could possibly want.

In Summary...

- The PSAT/NMSQT is a standardized test that high school sophomores and juniors usually take. Its purpose is to give a student a sense of how they will do on the SAT or ACT and to determine if they will qualify for the National Merit Scholarship process.

- The SAT and ACT are the two major standardized tests that most American colleges expect applicants to have taken. Higher scores translate to better odds of getting into selective colleges.

- The TOEFL is a standardized test that students who do not speak English as their primary language usually have to take in order to be considered for admission at English-speaking colleges like those in the United States.

- Colleges are becoming more flexible about applicants' submitting SAT and ACT scores. Some colleges don't require them at all nowadays. However, every college accepts them, and a high SAT or ACT score will make you a more competitive college applicant.

- An AP exam is an end-of-year, standardized test that measures a student's command of material in a certain AP course. High AP exam scores can make you a more competitive college applicant and even lead to college course credit.

- SAT Subject Tests, also referred to as SAT II, are subject-specific, standardized tests that high school students can choose to take to show their strength in particular academic areas. They are usually not required, but they can set an applicant apart.

Finding Colleges That Fit

Check for Accreditation

A restaurant can't open until it passes a health inspection, during which a trained inspector makes sure it's a safe place for food to be cooked and eaten. Only then can it serve customers. Passing a health inspection is not an achievement; it's the bare minimum for a restaurant to stay in business.

While a restaurant goes through a health inspection, each college must go through a process called "accreditation." Like a health inspector, an accrediting agency evaluates the college to make sure it's a place students can receive a legitimate education. There are no levels of accreditation; a college is accredited or not, and not being accredited is a bad thing. Accreditation is not an achievement; it's the bare minimum for a college to be considered acceptable.

Be careful! A restaurant cannot open until it passes a health inspection. A college, on the other hand, *can* operate without having been through the accreditation process. **Do not** apply to or attend an unaccredited college.

Attending an accredited college means:

- The academic programs offered by the school are at least acceptable.
- Potential employers will take your degree seriously.
- If you have financial need, you will be eligible to receive federal financial aid.
- Your tuition will qualify for federal income tax deductions and/or other tax credits.
- If you transfer to another accredited college, your academic credits will go with you.

Just because a college is accredited, it DOES NOT mean that:

- You will definitely receive financial aid; this depends on need.
- You will receive an education equal in quality to the educations offered at all other accredited colleges.
- The academic credits you earn at one school will count toward the graduation requirements at another school if you transfer.

How to check if a college is accredited:

Visit ope.ed.gov/accreditation/ for the U.S. Department of
Education's database of accredited postsecondary institutions. You
can also check out the Council for Higher Education Accreditation at
www.chea.org.

Advice for the College Search

Before you start building your college list, I would love for you to <u>consider</u> the following tidbits of advice. I think, if you heed them, you'll make better choices!

- **Be open-minded:** There are thousands of incredible colleges out there. Some are in places you've never heard of or been to. Open your mind to the <u>vast</u> opportunities. It will pay off.

- **No perfect college:** There are over 3,000 colleges where you can get a four-year degree. Of those, there are several hundred where you could be happy, do well, and graduate. This process is about fit, and you can fit well lots of places.

- **One college is for many types of people:** Two people with different backgrounds, personalities, interests, and goals can attend the same college and be equally successful. Each college offers a range of opportunities that <u>cater</u> to many different types of students.

- **Some Colleges Are Good, and Some Are Less Good:** There is no perfect college, but there are colleges where your chances of success will be higher. Knowing what makes some colleges good and others less good will help you narrow your list.

- **You better work:** I'm doing my best to steer you in the right direction, but it's sort of up to you to steer yourself. You will have to do research to find schools that could be a good fit for you.

- **Focusing on cost alone can cost you:** Never rule out a college because of its cost of attendance, also known as "sticker price." Some of the most expensive colleges can be the cheapest to attend. Sounds weird. Trust me. More later.

- **Not focusing on cost can cost you:** You never want to be in a position in which you can't afford any of the colleges on your list. To avoid that <u>unenviable</u> position, add 1-2 financial safety schools. More on this later.

- **<u>Embrace</u> uncertainty:** In the process of building your college list and eventually choosing a school, you may never feel certain. If you do your research, you will make <u>informed</u> choices, and things should work out okay—great even.

How to Build a College List

It kills me to tell you there is no formula for building a college list. Instead I'm offering two approaches I think can be useful, whether you don't know where to begin or have a clear sense of direction. Either approach, or both simultaneously, could lead to the college list you seek.

Regardless the approach you choose, you should be able to answer "yes" to three screening questions before adding any college to your list:

1. **Can I get in?** - Apply to schools you have at least a shot of getting accepted to. More on this later.

2. **Can I afford it?** - Apply to schools your family can pay for responsibly. But first you need to know how paying for college works. More on this later.

3. **Can I succeed here?** - Apply to schools that will provide a high-quality education. See "What Makes a College Good?" for more information.

Now, let's get back to our two approaches...

The Targeted Approach

Determine what you want in a college, and search for schools that match those criteria. Here are some criteria many students care about:

1. **Academic Programs/Majors:** Some colleges are known for certain academic programs, like Xavier University of New Orleans' pre-pharmacy track. If you're certain of what you want to study, choosing colleges based on their academic programs is a good way to narrow your list.

2. **Diversity:** Some colleges do better than others bringing students from a variety of backgrounds to campus. If this matters to you (it should), factor it in.

3. **Location:** If you insist on attending college in a particular state or region, your search just got that much easier.

4. **Student Body:** If you have strong feelings about the number of students you want to go to college with, student body size can help you narrow your search.

5. **School Spirit:** Some colleges are known for passionate fans and supporters who bleed the school's colors. If that's your cup of tea, more power to you!

6. **Special Missions:** Examples include include arts colleges, historically Black colleges, religiously <u>affiliated</u> colleges, Hispanic-serving colleges, and more. If you feel a connection to a special mission, use it to focus your search.

Where do you search?

Besides colleges' homepages, there are many websites that will generate lists of schools based on criteria you enter. These "matchmaking" sites are valuable but <u>imperfect</u>. Not even the most <u>sophisticated</u> technology could show you all options that are a good fit. That's where our second approach, Exploratory, comes in handy.

Examples of College Matchmaking Sites

- <u>bigfuture.collegeboard.org</u>
- <u>www.collegedata.com</u>
- <u>www.collegexpress.com</u>
- <u>nces.ed.gov/collegenavigator</u>
- <u>www.collegeresults.org</u>
- <u>www.unigo.com</u>

The Exploratory Approach

Whereas the Targeted Approach starts with limits (i.e. criteria) to define your college search, the Exploratory Approach relies on broad discovery to gradually find strong-fit colleges.

Here's a helpful analogy. I love listening to music, but I'm not always looking for a specific song. Sometimes I just want to hear music that fits my current vibe. Thank goodness the music-playing app Spotify offers playlists for various moods. If I'm trying to take the edge off after a hard day's work, for instance, I might throw on the "evening chill" playlist. I usually come across 2-3 songs I'd never heard that I end up adding to my library. In fact, "evening chill" is where I discovered the song my wife and I had our first dance to!

The Exploratory Approach lets students stretch their thinking and create a vision for themselves before setting the limits that will define their college search. By exploring "playlists" of schools that have something important, but general, in common, students can find new schools that fit what they're looking for.

Here are some examples:

- **Colleges That Change Lives (www.ctcl.org):** Member schools are small, liberal arts colleges and universities with high rates of student success.

- **Most Generous Colleges:** Google this to see the colleges that provide the most robust financial aid packages. They tend to be tough to get into.

- **CollegeXpress:** Use the "Lists and Rankings" feature to find colleges grouped in a variety of ways. There are over 800 lists!

- **Coalition for Access, Affordability, and Success:** Member colleges and universities are committed to college access for underrepresented students.

There is no formula. Building a college list takes a bit of science and a bit of art. I recommend a healthy combination of the Targeted and Exploratory approaches, while making sure you run each school through the three screen questions. Do that and you should end up with a strong college list. If you don't, pretend this never happened.

First, Can You Get In?

In "How to Build a College List," I told you that, before adding a college to your list, you should be able to answer "yes" to the question: can I get in?

Each college application you submit takes <u>considerable</u> time and energy. You should only spend time and energy applying to schools that you have a shot of getting accepted to.

Some colleges are harder to get into than others. The harder a college is to get into, the more "selective" it is. Stanford University, which admits just 5% of its applicants, is more selective than Hampton University, which accepts 70% of its applicants. Wabash College, on the other hand, accepts 100% of its applicants.

The strength of your Big Five—GPA, ACT/SAT, involvement, essays, and recommendation letters—will determine how competitive you are to get into certain schools. The college application process is a game of chance with no guarantees. You need to play the odds by applying to 9–12 schools; some will be sure bets and others more of a gamble. Break your list into three groups based on your chances of getting accepted:

- **Safety (3 schools):** A "safety" school is one where your GPA and SAT/ACT are well above the averages for incoming freshmen. It's a school that will almost certainly accept you. 1–2 of these schools should be *financial* safety schools, colleges you know you and your family will be able to afford.

- **Target (6 schools):** A "target" school is one where your GPA and SAT/ACT are <u>on par</u> with the averages for incoming freshmen.

- **Reach (3 schools):** A "reach" school is one where your GPA and SAT/ACT are below the averages for incoming freshmen, but you have reason to believe the <u>totality</u> of your application (essays, involvement, recommendation letters, etc.) still gives you a shot at admission. Be honest with yourself when a school is out of your range and would be a waste of time to apply to.

When it comes to big universities that don't care about anything besides an applicant's GPA and ACT/SAT, your chances of acceptance should be clear. It's a different story for colleges with a holistic admissions process (meaning they care about factors other than GPA and ACT/SAT). These colleges might accept an applicant whose GPA and ACT/SAT are below average but whose other application components are inspiring.

If you follow the advice above and create a thoughtful, balanced college list, you will be set up to responsibly play the odds—to shoot for the stars while having a couple backup plans.

What Makes a College Good?

I believe you can find success at almost any college. Some colleges, though, are better <u>equipped</u> than others to support their students and to make sure they are prepared for what comes after graduation, academically and non-academically.

The four "indicators" below are linked to student learning and growth. Colleges that are strong in all four almost always have high graduation rates and success with job and graduate school placement. In other words, their students are almost always successful.

These indicators come from the National Survey of Student Engagement (NSSE), which has identified that you want to attend a college with the following:

1. Academic Rigor

You want a college where you'll have to work hard to earn good grades. When researching, look for:

- **Higher-order learning:** Students complete complex work rather than memorize facts.
- **<u>Reflective</u> and integrative learning:** Students connect what they learn in class to personal experiences and current events.
- **Learning strategies:** Students engage with course material outside of class by reviewing notes, identifying key info in readings, and more.
- **<u>Quantitative</u> reasoning:** Students improve math skills so they can use numerical information in everyday life.

2. Learning with Peers

You want a college where students share what they learn with others, exchange ideas and perspectives, and <u>collaborate</u> on work.

- **Collaborative learning:** Students work together on assignments and when studying for exams.
- **Diversity:** Students have plenty of discussions, in and out of class, with peers from different backgrounds.

3. Experiences with Faculty

You want a college where students interact regularly with their professors, in and out of class.

- **Student-faculty <u>interaction</u>:** Professors are available to discuss course concepts, academic performance, career plans, and general concerns.

- **Effective teaching practices:** Professors clearly explain course goals and requirements, provide detailed feedback, and break down hard concepts.

4. Campus Environment

You want a campus environment that's academically and socially supportive and where students are highly engaged.

- **Staff interactions:** Students have positive interactions with academic advisors, student services, and administrators (e.g. financial aid)

- **Beyond-class engagement:** Students are engaged in a <u>multitude</u> of activities and events outside of class.

- **Student services:** Students have access to services, like tutoring, that will help them succeed academically.

- **Peer engagement:** Students have plenty of chances to get involved socially and interact with peers from different backgrounds.

The information above is not a checklist and, if it was, no college would tick every box. Rather it's meant to guide your thinking as you look for schools where you would likely succeed. For further help, check out NSSE's free "Pocket Guide to Choosing a College," which offers questions that can help you determine how strong a college is in each of the four indicators.

What Makes a College Bad?

When choosing a college, it's as important to know what to seek out as it is to know what to avoid. Let's keep it simple: Be wary of colleges where students are likely to leave before graduating, take on heavy debt, or both.

Debt is money you owe. We'll discuss later that many students take out loans to pay for college. They're making <u>investments</u> in their futures that they expect will pay off later when they graduate, get jobs, and start making money (which they'll use to pay back their loans). Whether the investment pays off depends, at least in part, on the college one attends.

Let's look at some of these "red flags." While most are not deal-breakers, they are warning signs that should give you cause to pause:

- **No accreditation:** This one actually *is* a deal-breaker. Remember that accreditation is a college's health inspection, the bare minimum to be considered legitimate. Avoid unaccredited colleges or those that have struggled to remain accredited.

- **Low freshmen retention rate:** This is the proportion of freshmen who return sophomore year. A low rate may mean students aren't well-supported or that many are generally unsatisfied. Whatever the cause, be wary of schools where most students leave after one year.

- **Low graduation rate:** This is the proportion of students who earn bachelor's degrees. A low graduation rate can mean lots of things, none of them good. The goal of college is to graduate. Whatever the causes, be wary of schools were most students don't.

- **Low graduation rate for Pell-eligible students:** Colleges award Pell Grants—a type of federal financial aid—to students who need assistance paying for school. If you fall in this category, be wary of schools where most lower-income students drop out.

- **High <u>cohort</u> default rate:** Default happens when you can't pay back loans. A high "cohort default" rate indicates many students are incurring heavy debt to afford college, but they're either not graduating or not securing jobs upon graduation. Defaulting on loans has serious consequences we will discuss later.

- **High average student debt ($30,000 or more):** Avoid schools where the average student is incurring monstrous debt to pay for school.

You want to attend a college you can responsibly pay for and where you are likely to graduate with a degree that will lead to jobs. As you're considering schools, be wary of anything that could <u>prevent</u> that.

Types of Colleges

In America there are more than 4,000 two- and four-year post-secondary institutions. There are three types of post-secondary colleges:

1. **Undergraduate two-year college:**
   - Usually comes right after high school
   - Also known as community college or junior college
   - Earn an associate degree or skill certificate upon graduation

2. **Undergraduate four-year college/university:**
   - Usually comes right after high school
   - Undergraduates have many different options for their studies
   - Earn a bachelor's degree upon graduation

3. **Graduate School:**
   - Comes after four-year college but not necessarily right after
   - Has a specific professional focus like medicine, law, business
   - Earn a master's or doctoral degree, or both, upon graduation

This section is focused on four-year colleges and universities. Throughout this book, I use the term "college" to refer to all four-year, post-secondary schools. However, in this section, and as you think about your own college search, it's important to understand the difference between a college and university.

University

Examples: University of Virginia, University of Wisconsin-Madison

- Usually larger, both in campus and student body size
- Usually broken into smaller "colleges" based on area of study
  - Ex: At Louisiana State University, undergraduates can earn degrees from the College of Business, College of Engineering, etc.
- Usually offer graduate degrees in addition to undergraduate degrees
- Class sizes usually larger; students may receive less attention from professors
- Usually more options for majors than at a college

College

In this case, I mean a standalone school, not a college within a university.

Examples: Spelman College, Bates College, Amherst College, Morehouse College

- Usually smaller, both in campus and student body size
- Not broken up into smaller "colleges" or "schools" based on area of study
- Students can still choose from a variety of majors and classes
- Usually do not offer graduate degrees; focus is on undergraduate education

Now you know that a four-year postsecondary institution can be characterized either as a college or university, depending on the traits listed above. The next thing to understand is that not all colleges and not all universities are the same. Let's now look at different types of colleges and universities.

- **Liberal arts colleges** are not preoccupied with students preparing for a particular career track. Rather, they want their students to explore many subjects, gain a broad base of knowledge and skills, and become creative and critical thinkers. A liberal arts college can stand on its own (e.g., Pomona College) or be a college within a university (e.g., University of Pennsylvania's College of Arts and Sciences).

- **Arts colleges** focus on the arts. Apart from traditional coursework (math, science, languages, etc.), there is training on specific arts disciplines such as photography, music, theater, fashion, graphic design, and more. An arts college can stand on its own (e.g., Rhode Island School of Design) or be a college within a university (e.g., University of Michigan's Stamps School of Art & Design).

- **Religiously affiliated colleges/universities** are connected to a religious faith. The connection may or may not be a big part of daily student life. You'll have to find that out for yourself. Examples: Brigham Young University (Mormon), Southern Methodist University (Methodist), and Yeshiva University (Jewish).

- **Historically Black Colleges/Universities (HBCUs)** were created at a time when black students were not allowed to attend most other colleges. Their mission is the education of black students. Non-black students are allowed to attend, but it is not common. Examples: Morehouse College, Spelman College, Tuskegee University, Fisk University, and Morgan State University.

- **Hispanic-Serving Colleges/Universities (HACUs)** have at least a quarter of their undergraduate population made up of Hispanic students. Examples: Arizona Western College, University of Arizona South, and California State University, Chico.

- **Single-sex colleges** are gender identity-specific, meaning they are either for men or for women. They are not coeducational, like most colleges are. Examples: Agnes Scott College (women), Wellesley College (women), Morehouse College (men & HBCU), Spelman College (women & HBCU).

Don't get caught up in the labels; there will not be a quiz! Focus on differences that matter to you. If you don't want to attend school with more than 1,000 students, steer clear of universities. If you want a career in fashion design or photography, consider an arts college. Understanding the major differences between types of colleges will help you make more informed choices when you're building your list.

Types of Degrees

Here are several degrees you can earn and what types of schools you need to graduate from to earn them.

High School Diploma:

- Offered by your high school
- A General Educational Development Test (GED) is <u>equivalent</u>
- **Why get one?** Set yourself up to enter some kind of post-secondary education. While graduating high school is awesome, it should not be the finish line. Having only a high school diploma will offer limited job options.

Associate Degree:

- Community or career colleges offer this degree
- Usually requires 60 credit hours, or two years, of coursework
- Some people transfer afterward to a four-year college (Transfer Associate Degree); others start working (Occupational Associate Degree)
- **Why get one?** It's a good option when four-year college doesn't make sense. Plenty of great jobs require an associate degree, but *only* having an associate degree may limit your career options and ability to rise through the ranks and make more money.

Bachelor's Degree:

- Four-year colleges and universities offer this degree
- Students earn a Bachelor of Art (BA) or Bachelor of Science (BS)
- **Why get one?** It will typically offer you more professional options than an associate degree will. Having a bachelor's also gives you the option for graduate school, which leads to even more professional opportunities.

Graduate/Advanced Degree:

- Graduate schools offer this degree
- Usually completed after bachelor's; joint degree programs may allow a student to pursue a bachelor's and graduate degree at the same time.
- Each graduate program has a focus (e.g., social work, education, business, etc.) and will be more challenging than bachelor's degree work.

- Graduate degree can be either a master's, which usually takes two years, or a doctorate, which can take up to four years (or more).
- **Why get one?** Further your education, increase your job prospects, and set yourself up to earn more money. Some professions, like being a college professor, require advanced degrees.

Professional Degree:

- Some professions are not available unless you have a specific professional degree
- For instance, you can't become a doctor, nurse, physician's assistant, or lawyer without obtaining the required professional degree
- Some professional degrees can be earned at the undergraduate level (e.g., teaching); others require <u>extensive</u> graduate studies (e.g., medicine)
- **Why get one?** Your desired career requires one!

Major FAQs

What is a major?

A major is a focus for your college studies. Not all your classes will be tied to your major, but the bulk of them will.

What are some examples of majors?

There are thousands, and each school offers different ones. Examples include: History, Psychology, Biology, Accounting, Chemical Engineering, Art History, African-American Studies, Exercise Science, and more. The list is literally never-ending. Some colleges even let you invent your own.

When do I have to decide on a major?

Different colleges have different deadlines for declaring a major, but it's usually after sophomore year. You don't need to enter college certain of your major. In fact I urge you to be open-minded. College is about academic exploration.

What if I want to go to graduate school? Does my major matter then?

No. As long as you complete the undergraduate courses your graduate program requires, you can major in anything you want. In fact, many graduate schools like to see non-obvious majors. For example, a friend of mine got accepted to a top medical school, and his undergraduate major was Art History.

Do all students in the same major take the same courses and study the same things?

No. Colleges offer a wide range of courses within one major, and students in that major can have completely different focuses for their studies. Just be aware if there are required courses for all students in a specific major.

Once I choose a major, can I change it?

Yes. The vast majority of college students change their major, sometimes more than once. Ask people you know with bachelor's degrees. You'll find most changed their majors or considered it.

How is a minor different from a major?

A minor is a <u>secondary</u> academic interest, whereas your major is your <u>primary</u> academic focus. Completing a minor requires fewer credits than graduating with a major. You cannot graduate with a minor alone.

What is double majoring?

It's what it sounds like: having two majors. If you want to double major, get on track early. You will, of course, have more required courses to complete.

How do I choose a major?

Most students choose majors that connect with the line of work they intend to <u>pursue</u> after college. This makes sense but doesn't have to be your rule of thumb. I recommend you pick a major you're passionate about so you're motivated to work hard.

How Important Is My Major?

If you're certain of what you want to be when you grow up, it's smart to enter college with an idea of how your studies will connect to your desired career. First, this can help you narrow your college search. Second, you can make sure you're taking college courses in which you'll build valuable skills for your chosen field. For example, if you want to be a mechanical engineer, your math game will need to be strong. Finally, if you enter college knowing you want to attend a certain graduate school, you can begin right away taking courses required to participate in the desired program.

If you're *not* certain what you want to be when you grow up, you're not alone. Actually you're in the majority. Many students believe they must choose a major before choosing a college and that major must match perfectly with career <u>aspirations</u> they're currently unsure of. There are four problems with this belief.

First, asking a student to choose a career path before college is like asking someone to order before seeing the menu. College is a chance to explore your interests. As you take different courses, learn from peers and mentors, and engage with new experiences, a vision for your professional future will <u>gradually</u> take shape, and even then it likely won't be exact or final.

Second, majors don't match perfectly with careers. Yes, some <u>align</u> better with certain professions than with others. If someone wanted to become a nurse, it would make more sense for them to major in nursing than history. But most jobs don't match so obviously with majors. It's not that simple.

Third, no one can predict how a career will unfold, especially today, when people change jobs much more frequently than they used to. Many college graduates enter the workforce in fields unrelated to their degrees. It may take several years before you land your "dream job." By then the tide of life may have caused you to drift far from where you imagined your major would take you. That's not necessarily a bad thing.

Fourth and finally, a college education is <u>comprised</u> of many learning experiences, just one of which is your major coursework. You will take courses outside your major, perform research, hold jobs and internships, participate in activities beyond class, and dig into campus life. How deeply you engage with the various aspects of your college experience is what will determine your readiness for what comes after graduation.

That's the point: what you major in is less important than *how* you major in it. If you challenge yourself academically, any major can be valuable and prepare you for a wide range of professions. Major in what interests you. Go hard at it. But don't stop there. Find commitments outside class that make you come alive and keep you busy. If you follow this advice, you will gain skills and experiences that will make you competitive for many jobs, and you will graduate with a degree that's worth something.

You Can Do THAT in College?

College is so much cooler than high school. To get you pumped for it, I want to tell you some stuff you can do that you might not have imagined.

28 Fascinating College Courses

Remember, not all your college courses have to be within your major. You can take random ones that interest you. Check out this list. Each of these courses is currently being offered or was at one point.

- Beats, Rhyme & Life: Hip-Hop Studies – Wellesley College (Wellesley, MA)

- Create Your Own Religion – Alfred University (Alfred, NY)

- Death in Perspective – Kean University (Union, NJ)

- Demystifying the Hipster – Tufts University (Somerville, MA)

- Politicizing Beyoncé – Rutgers University (New Brunswick, NJ)

- Gossip – Cornell University (Ithaca, NY)

- How to Win a Beauty Pageant – Oberlin College (Oberlin, Ohio)

- Ice Cream Short Course – Pennsylvania State University (University Park, PA)

- Japanese Swordsmanship – George Washington University (Washington, D.C.)

- Lady Gaga & the Sociology of Fame – University of South Carolina (Columbia, SC)

- Learning From YouTube – Pitzer College (Claremont, CA)

- Life – Yale University (New Haven, CT)

- Philosophy & Star Trek – Georgetown University (Washington, D.C.)

- Psychology, Biology & Politics of Food – Yale University (New Haven, CT)

- Strategy of StarCraft – University of California at Berkeley (Berkeley, CA)

- Street-Fighting Mathematics – Massachusetts Institute of Technology (Cambridge, MA)

- Stupidity – Occidental University (Los Angeles, CA)

- Tattoos in American Popular Culture – Pitzer College (Claremont, CA)
- The Art of Walking – Centre College (Danville, KY)
- The Game of Thrones – University of Virginia (Charlottesville, VA)
- The Hunger Games: Class, Politics & Marketing – American University (Washington, D.C.)
- The Joy of Garbage – Santa Clara University (Santa Clara, CA)
- The Science of Harry Potter – Frostburg State University (Frostburg, MD)
- The Science of Superheroes – University of California at Irvine (Irvine, CA)
- The Simpsons & Philosophy – University of California at Berkeley (Berkeley, CA)
- The Textual Appeal of Tupac Shakur – University of Washington (Seattle, WA)
- Whiteness: The Other Side of Racism – Mount Holyoke College (South Hadley, MA)
- Zombies in Popular Media – Columbia College (Chicago, IL)

10 Interesting College Clubs & Organizations

In college, as much or more learning takes place outside class as in it. Below are some examples of interesting clubs and organizations at colleges across the country.

- Cheese Club – SUNY Purchase (Purchase, NY)
- Clown Nose Club – North Carolina State University (Raleigh, NC)
- Concrete Canoe Club – University of Wisconsin-Madison (Madison, WI)
- Dignified Educated United Crust Eaters Society – Western Michigan University (Kalamazoo, MI)
- Happiness Club – Northwestern University (Evanston, IL)
- People Watching People – University of Minnesota (Minneapolis, MN)
- Rock, Papers, Scissors Club – University of Kentucky (Lexington, KY)
- Sky Diving Club – Virginia Tech (Blacksburg, VA)
- Squirrel Club – University of Michigan (Ann Arbor, MI)
- Wizards & Muggles – College of William & Mary (Williamsburg, VA)

15 Awesome College Majors

College is a chance to explore your academic interests as you begin forming a vision for your professional future. Can you imagine yourself pursuing any of the unique majors below?

- Adventure Education – Plymouth State University (Plymouth, NH)
- Arctic Engineering – University of Alaska Fairbanks (Fairbanks, AK)
- Astrobiology (life outside of earth) – University of Washington (Seattle, WA)
- Bakery Science – Kansas State University (Manhattan, KS)
- Bowling Industry Management & Technology – Vincennes University (Vincennes, IN)
- Citrus – Florida Southern College (Lakeland, FL)
- Egyptology – Brown University (Providence, RI)
- Entertainment Engineering and Design – University of Nevada (Las Vegas, NV)
- Exercise and Movement Sciences – University of Vermont (Burlington, VM)
- Fermentation Science – Colorado State University (Fort Collins, CO)
- Floral Management – Mississippi State University (Mississippi State, MS)
- Pop Culture – Western Kentucky University (Bowling Green, KY)
- Therapeutic Horsemanship – St. Andrews University (Laurinburg, NC)
- Toy Design – Otis College of Art and Design (Los Angeles, CA)
- Viticulture & Enology (study of wine) – Cornell University (Ithaca, NY)

7 Incredible Study Abroad Programs

"Studying abroad" means spending a semester or summer studying and living in another country. Everyone I know who has studied abroad describes it as life-changing! Check out these incredible programs offered by colleges in the United States and overseas.

- Antarctica: The Fragile Continent – University of Georgia (Athens, GA)
- Abu Dhabi – New York University (New York, NY)
- Venice, Italy Campus – Wake Forest (Winston-Salem, NC)

- Summer in Scandinavia – Harvard University (Cambridge, MA)

- Semester at Sea (explore on a cruise ship) – offered to students at any college

- Argentina Tango Arts & Cultural Immersion – Texas A&M University (College Station, TX)

- Eat & Make Gelato – Carpigiani Gelato University (Italy)

We're just scratching the surface! College is about exploring what makes you come alive, in and out of class, and then digging deep into those passions. I hope this article gives you a sense of the possibilities awaiting you.

Demonstrate Interest

Colleges want to feel the love. If they want you, they want you to want them back. They also would prefer not to offer one of their limited spots to a student who will likely enroll somewhere else.

This is why more and more schools care about "demonstrated interest," which is just what it sounds like: how much you show a college you want to go there.

Not all colleges care about demonstrated interest. For those that do, its importance in the admissions process can range from "considered" to "very important." Here are some examples of colleges that value demonstrate interest to different <u>extents</u>.

How much does demonstrated interest factor into admissions decisions?		
Considered	**Important**	**Very Important**
Barnard College	Auburn University	American University
Colby College	Austin College	Dickinson College
Colorado College	Bates College	Olin College of
Connecticut College	Boston University	Engineering
Grinnell College	Brandeis University	Hillsdale College
Hamilton College	Carnegie Mellon	Ithaca College
Haverford College	University	Morehouse College
Middlebury College	DePaul University	Pacific University
Mount Holyoke College	Eckerd College	Quinnipiac University
New York University	Florida Institute of Tech.	Skidmore College
Oberlin College	Reed College	Syracuse University
Rice University	Roanoke College	U.S. Air Force
Trinity College	Seton Hall University	Academy
Tufts University	University of Arizona	U.S. Naval Academy
Villanova University	University of Dayton	Wabash College
	University of Tulsa	Webb Institute
		Westmont College

How to Demonstrate Interest

Enough colleges care about demonstrated interest for you to know about it and use it to your advantage. If one of the schools you plan to apply to values demonstrated interest, here are some concrete ways to show love:

- **Write a great "why us?" essay** – Many colleges require an essay that asks why you want to attend. This is your chance to show your passion for the school.

- **Visit campus** – Many colleges keep track of students who visit and attend admissions information sessions. If you can't afford the trip, see if the school has special programs that pay for interested students to visit.

- **Attend recruitment events** – Many colleges host recruitment events for high school students, like overnight visits, preview days, and more. These are great chances to learn more about a school while demonstrating interest.

- **Choose to interview** – Though college interviews are mainly optional, I recommend you see them as an opportunity. Interviews are chances to further <u>humanize</u> your written application, and they're also a way to show sincere interest.

- **Attend college fairs** – The representatives who <u>facilitate</u> tables at college fairs are often the admissions officers who will decide whether to let you in. Have <u>meaningful</u> discussions with them, leave your name and contact info, and take their business cards so you can reach out to them if you have more questions.

- **Send thank-you notes** – If you have a good discussion with a representative at a college fair, it's nice to follow up with a thank-you note. The same is true if you have an interview. Handwritten is best, but an email would <u>suffice</u>.

- **Email your admissions officer** – If you are genuinely interested in attending a college, it doesn't hurt to send an email to the admissions officer for your state or region. The email is a chance to introduce yourself, express interest, ask questions, and request additional information.

- **Connect through social media** – Sign up for and participate on colleges' blogs, follow them on Twitter and Instagram, and "like" their Facebook pages.

- **Use your FAFSA** – If you're sure about your top-choice college, list it first when you indicate the schools you want your FAFSA to be sent to. Otherwise list your colleges in alphabetical order so no college appears to be your favorite.

- **Apply early** – Applying Early Decision is the ultimate demonstration of interest because an Early Decision acceptance <u>binds</u> you to attending. Applying Early Action also shows <u>notable eagerness</u> to attend a school.

Tips for Demonstrating Interest

- **Don't be afraid, nervous, embarrassed, or ashamed.** Many students don't want to demonstrate interest. They see it as stalking or sucking up. It's not that. It's putting your best foot forward. There's no shame in that game.

- **Ask thoughtful, specific questions.** Ask questions that couldn't be answered by looking on the college's website. Also, avoid <u>generic</u> questions that could be asked of any school. Thoughtful questions specific to the college will show <u>authentic</u> interest.

- **Don't badger.** Know when enough is enough. If you incessantly contact a college admissions officer, you'll stand out in the wrong way: for being <u>vexing</u> and <u>inauthentic</u>.

- **Spread the love.** There are many ways to demonstrate interest. Utilize a variety. Multiple touch points will show a more sincere and complete interest.

What You Need to Know About Greek Life

If a college has "Greek Life," it means it has fraternities and/or sororities. A fraternity, or "frat," is a student organization only for men, while a sorority is one only for women. How important Greek Life is will vary from campus to campus.

What They're About

Different types of fraternities and sororities have different focuses:

- **Social:** Focused on bringing people together to have fun. Social fraternities and sororities may get involved in other campus and community initiatives.

- **Academic:** Focused on bringing together students who have a shared commitment to doing well in school and growing as scholars.

- **Multicultural:** May combine aspects of academic and social Greek Life. Usually bring together students from similar cultural, racial, or ethnic backgrounds.

- **All the above:** Some houses have social, academic, multicultural, and other focuses wrapped in one. It just depends on the fraternity/sorority.

Benefits of Joining

Whether the focus is social, academic, multicultural, all the above, or something totally different, joining a fraternity or sorority can be awesome for several reasons:

- **Expand your circle:** Greek life is a great way to meet friends. "Brothers" and "sisters" build strong relationships that turn into lifelong bonds.

- **Community:** It's important in college to have a community that makes you feel at home. A Greek organization can give you a social hub and sense of belonging.

- **Career connections:** Relationships you build can help you in the job hunt. If you join a Greek organization that has a national network, you can connect with thousands of brothers or sisters across the country.

- **Involvement:** Greek organizations participate in initiatives on campus and in the surrounding community. These are great chances to have fun, do good, develop new skills, and beef up your professional résumé.

- **Leadership:** Holding a leadership role within a Greek organization—such as president, treasurer, social chair, etc.—can make you a more attractive job candidate and better prepare you for the professional world.

Potential <u>Drawbacks</u> of Joining

- **Hazing:** Many Greek organizations force new recruits to complete challenges to earn their spots. Hazing can range from humiliating to harmful. It can even be <u>fatal</u>. Avoid Greek organizations that will not treat you decently.

- **Distraction:** If you don't manage your time effectively, being in a fraternity or sorority can distract you from more important priorities like schoolwork.

- **Money:** Some Greek organizations require expensive dues from their members. Some students simply can't afford to participate.

- **Rules:** To be in a fraternity or sorority, you may have to abide by strict rules and meet certain standards. If that's not your thing, this could be a bad fit.

- **Other dangers:** Do your research. Don't join a Greek organization that is known for questionable behavior and will push you to engage in the same. Rather join one that will be fun and push you to be a better person and student.

Maximize College Tours

We've all been in a situation where a friend told us a story and it turned out we "had to be there" to appreciate it. College is like that. To really get it, you have to be there. That's where college tours come in. A college tour is important for getting a firsthand, real-life sense of what a certain school is like.

Why go

- Feel what life at the college is really like
- See how students spend time, and learn what they like and dislike
- Gather key info to make your final college decision
- College tours count as demonstrated interest

When to go

- **Junior year -** Determine your likes and dislikes before creating your college tour list.
- **Weekday -** Go when normal classes are in session.
- **After you're accepted -** This is more of a luxury, but it helps you make final decisions.
- **Less good times to go:**
  o Summer, when the campus will be dead
  o During exams, move-in week, graduation, and any other time you wouldn't be able to see what an average day is like

Before the tour

- **Get your mind right:** On a college tour, you are an investigator. Remind yourself that the trip is about gathering information, not goofing off with friends.
- **Plan, but don't overplan:** Create an itinerary for each school, but leave enough free time to casually explore campus.
- **Do research:** Read about each school beforehand. Coming in with prior knowledge improves learning.
- **Prepare questions:** Go in with questions ready. I've provided some examples on the next few pages, but I encourage you to come up with your own.
- **Prepare materials:** Bring a pen and something to take notes on.

During the tour

- **Focus:** Put your phone on airplane mode. Listen attentively and ask questions. Fight off exhaustion; you can rest later.

- **Make good impressions:** If people on campus remember you after you have left, make sure it's for good things.

- **Document:** Take thorough notes. Take pics and videos with your phone. Jot down contact information of students or staff you interact with.

After the tour

- **Reflect collaboratively:** We learn by reflecting on our experiences. After each tour, exchange your thoughts and feelings with others.

- **Self-reflect:** Independently review notes, pictures, videos, etc. Replay the experience in your head. Write about your overall impression of each college. Do it immediately, or you will forget!

- **Show gratitude:** Send thank-you emails or handwritten notes to any staff members or students you interacted with. Here's an example of what you could say. Try to make it unique by referring to specific conversations or events that happened while you were there.

Dear (person's name)

I am writing to say thank you for taking time to make my visit to (college name) so great. The campus is amazing, but getting to speak with you really gave me a strong, intimate sense for the school. I am returning home with strong motivation to apply. One day, maybe I will be lucky enough to call (college name) my home. Thanks again!

Sincerely,

(your name)

College Visit To-Do List

There's so much you can include in a college visit. Here's a list of some valuable ways to spend your time. You can't do them all, so pick ones you have time for and feel would best help you to get a feel for the school. Remember to leave time for <u>aimless</u> wandering.

- Take a formal tour organized by the admissions office (set up in advance)

- Attend a formal information session (set up in advance; part of formal tour)

- Have an interview with an admissions officer (set up in advance)
- Visit a few classes; small classes may require prior permission
- Meet with a professor in an academic area that interests you (set up in advance)
- Athletes: meet with a coach and/or athlete in your sport (set up in advance)
- Visit the career services center
- Eat a meal; visitors can often get vouchers from the admissions office
- Check out restaurants or coffee shops that students like
- Read the school's newspaper
- Look at bulletin boards to see what activities and events are going on
- Check out the dorms (don't be embarrassed; just ask someone)
- Visit the college bookstore
- Visit the library, recreational/fitness center, and sports facilities
- Attend an event: sports, performing arts, debate, etc.

Making College Visits Affordable

It's understandable that many students do not go on college visits because they are too expensive. Here are some ideas to make them more affordable.

- **Fly-in programs:** Some colleges will pay for students to visit campus. A simple Google search will give you a list of those schools, or you can email your state's admissions officer to see if the school offers fly-ins.

- **Vouchers:** Not all colleges will pay for your travel, but many offer vouchers for food, travel, and hotels to help reduce costs while encouraging you to visit.

- **Scholarships:** There may be scholarships specifically to help students pay for college tours. Go look. It's time you started researching scholarships anyway!

- **Carpool:** If the schools are within driving distance, see if other peers/families would travel with you. Once you arrive, you can do your own thing if you choose.

- **Local visits:** Even if you don't want to attend local colleges, visiting them will give you ideas about what you like and don't like in a school.

- **Virtual tours:** Most schools offer virtual tours online. It's not as good as the real thing, but it's not a bad option either.

Questions to Ask on a College Tour

Below are a bunch of questions you could ask on a college tour. They are broken into categories based on what I have told you is important to look for in a college. Of course, you do not have to ask all of these.

Academics

You want a college that will push you academically.

- How much time do students usually spend studying or doing homework each week?
- On average, do students find courses challenging?
- How much reading and writing is expected?
- How often are students asked to make presentations?
- Do students have to use numbers or statistics throughout their coursework?

Collaboration

You want a college where you will get to work with and share ideas with others.

- How often do students work together on class projects and assignments?
- Do students usually work together in order to better understand the material?
- How often do students prepare for exams together?
- How often do students from different backgrounds interact?

Faculty

You want a college with professors who are supportive, available, and effective.

- Are faculty members available to support you when you need help?
- Do faculty members do a good job explaining course goals and requirements?
- Do faculty members give detailed feedback on assignments?
- Do faculty members support students with their future plans?
- Do faculty members ever work on projects with students?

- Do you ever interact with faculty outside of class?
- Are most classes taught by professors or by graduate students?

School Support

You want a college that provides the resources and services students need to succeed.

- Do students use learning support services, like writing coaching and tutoring?
- Does the school provide physical and mental health services?
- Are students satisfied with the academic advising services?
- Are students satisfied with the career support services?
- Do students get along with each other? Is the campus a friendly environment?
- What's the relationship like between students and school staff?
- Is the campus safe?

Campus Life

You want a college where life outside of class is <u>vibrant</u>.

- What do most students do for fun during the week and on weekends?
- Is there a lot of drinking and/or drug use on campus?
- Are most students involved in an activity outside of class?
- Are there plenty of school-sponsored events on campus?
- Is Greek Life a big thing on campus?

General Questions

You want a college that feels right.

- Are you happy you decided to come here?
- Have you experienced any pleasant or unpleasant surprises in your time here?
- What do you wish were different about this place?
- What advice would you give yourself when you were a freshman?

Maximize College Fairs

What is a college fair?

A college fair is a gathering of college recruiters and admissions officers who have come to tell high school students about the schools they represent. College fairs are usually held in a big space, like a basketball gym or large meeting room, where colleges can set up tables and students can walk around from one to the next.

Why are college fairs important?

College fairs are chances to learn about great schools you may not have heard of or be able to visit; they are opportunities to make good impressions on recruiters or admissions officers who may influence your admissions chances.

What do I need to do to prepare for a college fair?

- Before the fair, research the schools that interest you.
- Come to the fair with thoughtful questions you can't find answers to online. Take some ideas from the questions in "Maximize College Tours" on pages 99–100.
- Bring something to write with and on so you can take thorough notes.
- Dress professionally.
- Bring copies of your résumé to give to college representatives.

How do I maximize a college fair?

To "maximize" something means to make the most of it. Here's how:

- Pick a couple friends you can stroll around with, ones who will help keep you focused.
- Take notes while you speak to the college representatives!
- Fill out contact cards for schools you want to stay in touch with.
- Review your notes with a trusted friend, family member, or mentor afterward.
- Determine your next steps. What will you do with the info you learned?

How do I find a college fair?

Many high schools hold college fairs, but if yours doesn't, check the National Association for College Admission Counseling website for a list of fairs near you (www.nacacnet.org).

Do college fairs can count as "demonstrated interest?"

For the schools that care about demonstrated interest, the answer is yes! The women and men standing behind the tables are often the admissions officers who will read your applications and decide whether to accept you. Impressing them can only help you. Besides the advice in this section, here's how you can do that:

• Let college representatives know if you have applied or plan to

• Ask college representatives for their business cards

• The day after the fair, send emails or handwritten thank-you notes to all representatives you interacted with. Here's an example of what you might say (but try to make yours unique to your conversation with each one):

Dear (college representative),

It was great meeting you yesterday. I really appreciate you taking time to speak to me about (1-2 specific topics you discussed). Our conversation was very informative and only made me more confident in my plans to apply to (college name). I hope you have a safe trip back!

Sincerely,

(your name)

In Summary...

- Every school on your college list should be accredited—no exceptions!

- Put schools on your college list that have high graduation rates and low student debt. Also include safety schools, target schools, and reach schools.

- Go for the school that is going to make you a better person and lets you pursue the things you're passionate about.

- Take advantage of college tours and college fairs to get first-hand experience and ask the questions that are most important to you. This is the best way to see if a school is the right "fit" for you.

Applying to College

College Applications 101

To be considered for acceptance by any college, you must submit an application. Some colleges accept hard copy applications, but I strongly recommend applying online. Let's review the basics.

What does a college application usually ask for?

Not all college applications are the same, but here's what most ask for:

- **Personal info:** contact, <u>demographic</u>, and geographic information, citizenship status

- **Family info:** basic information about your parents and siblings

- **Education:** information about your high school, counselor, classes, grades, and academic awards

- **Testing:** standardized tests you've taken (e.g., ACT, SAT, SAT Subject, AP, etc.) and your scores from each one

- **Activities:** descriptions of what you've done outside class, including when and for how long

- **Financial aid:** indicate if you plan to apply for financial aid by submitting the FAFSA

- **Essays:** not always required, but when they are, they matter a lot; word counts and topics vary by school

- **Writing supplements:** additional, school-specific essays; not always required, but when they are, they matter a lot; word count and topic varies by school

- **Additional info:** section for you to add important information that you feel was not reflected <u>elsewhere</u> in your application

What goes with your application?

- **Application fee:** payments vary by college; students with financial need can secure waivers to bypass fees; but some schools don't accept waivers, even for students with financial need.

- **Official transcript:** document with all your high school classes and grades; counselor will provide this for you upon request.

- **Official SAT/ACT score report:** most colleges require submission of official SAT or ACT score reports, which you can arrange to be sent through The College Board or ACT Inc., respectively; different schools have different policies on score report submission, so pay close attention.

- **Other test scores:** students who take and do well on SAT II Subject Tests and/or AP exams should have their official score reports sent to their colleges through The College Board's website.

- **Recommendation letters:** letters from teachers, coaches, and mentors <u>vouching</u> for your character and commitment; not always required, but when they are, they matter a lot.

- **Auditions, portfolios, and supplementary materials:** samples of work usually submitted by performing artists who want to show colleges their <u>repertoires</u> of work visual artists may submit portfolios of work, recording artists may send in an audio file.

Application Tips

Keep this list handy as you complete your applications

- Stay organized; make sure you stay on top of different colleges' deadlines and requirements.

- Keep track of all your login information (passwords, PIN numbers, usernames).

- Save your work frequently. If not, you might get "timed out" and lose your work.

- Don't wait until the last minute to submit your applications. But will you really listen to me?

- Read directions thoroughly and follow them carefully.

- Type essays in MS Word or Google docs; once you're done, paste them into the application.

- Correctly capitalize and punctuate; avoid abbreviations; avoid lingo you'd use on social media. Note: this tip does not apply to your activity description.

- Before you click "submit," triple check for errors with a trusted mentor.

- After you click "submit," make sure you receive a confirmation email; if you don't, email the college.

A quick note about errors

Before you submit, make sure your application is error free. Remember, your application speaks for you. It's your little buddy going into admissions offices telling everyone you're awesome. If your little buddy is filled with <u>avoidable</u> errors, your little buddy looks sloppy and careless—and so do you. You don't want that. Your buddy doesn't want that. Take your time. Do it right.

Application Fee Waivers

Application fees can pile up. More and more platforms, like the Common Application, are allowing students who indicate they have financial need to <u>bypass</u> fees altogether. When that's not possible, financially eligible students can submit fee waivers from the National Association for College Admission Counseling (NACAC) in order to skip application fee payment.

Students typically get fee waivers from their high school counselors or a college access counselor at a community-based organization. In either case, an "authorized official" must approve the request before you can submit it. Counselors usually have a limited number of fee waivers, so you need to be proactive in securing them.

To learn more about fee waivers, including if you are eligible for one, visit: <u>www.nacacnet.org/studentinfo/feewaiver/pages/default.aspx</u>.

The Common Application and Others Like It

When the time comes, you will submit each of your college applications online using an electronic application platform (a fancy way of saying *website*). The platform you use will vary depending on the colleges you are applying to.

Most colleges request the same information, and it would be silly to rewrite everything for each college you apply to. That's why there are application portals that allow you to complete just one application and send it to a bunch of schools.

For this article, we are going to focus on The Common Application, but I am going to tell you about a few other application platforms that work the same way.

What is the Common Application?

The Common Application, also called the "Common App," is an online application platform accepted by more than 750 colleges. To see a list of these schools, visit www.commonapp.org, and click "Member Institutions." Again, the Common App lets you send the same application to numerous schools, cutting out repetitive work.

What do Common App schools have in common?

All Common App colleges use a "holistic" admissions process, meaning they don't just look at grades and test scores but also essays, recommendation letters, extracurricular involvement, and other qualitative components.

So I can really submit the exact same application to all my Common App schools?

Not exactly. The majority of your application, including your personal statement, will remain unchanged from school to school. However, many colleges require additional essays called "writing supplements." As with everything in the college application process, you need to pay close attention to each school's unique requirements. Here is an example of a writing supplement American University requires its applicants to complete:

How do you personally define an inclusive environment? What do you believe contributes to a diverse and accepting community? (400 words)

Wait, what's a personal statement?

All Common App schools ask for a personal statement, a longer essay (250-650 words) answering one of the available prompts. This essay is not school-specific; it's a part of the Common App, like your test scores or family information. Below are three of the seven Common App personal statement prompts from 2018-2019.

- *Some students have a background, identity, interest, or talent that is so meaningful they believe their application would be incomplete without it. If this sounds like you, then please share your story.*

- *The lessons we take from obstacles we encounter can be fundamental to later success. Recount a time when you faced a challenge, setback, or failure. How did it affect you, and what did you learn from the experience?*

- *Reflect on a time when you questioned or challenged a belief or idea. What prompted your thinking? What was the outcome?*

What other online application platforms work like the Common App?

There are many online application platforms where you can submit one application to various schools. Below are just a few examples.

- **Common Black College Application:** Accepted by more than 40 historically Black colleges and universities

- **The Coalition Application:** Accepted by 140 (and counting) member colleges, many of which also accept the Common App

- **University of California Application:** Required by all universities in the University of California system (like UC Berkeley, UC Irvine, etc.)

- **Apply Texas:** Accepted by public universities and a selection of private and community colleges throughout Texas

When and how should I create an account?

I recommend creating a Common App account at the end of your sophomore year so you can get a feel for it. Simply go to www.commonapp.org and click "Create an Account."

Do some colleges have their own application?

Sadly, yes. Some colleges do not participate on any application platform like I've described here. In those cases, you'll have to apply through the school's website.

The most frustrating part about the college application process is the lack of <u>uniformity</u>. Different colleges have different deadlines, accept different applications, and require different components. It's up to you to be aware of what each of your colleges is asking for. That's why staying organized is so key.

When to Apply

An "admission plan" refers to: 1) when you will apply to a certain college and 2) what it means if you are accepted there. I promise this will make more sense in a bit.

Different colleges offer different admissions plans. There are six you might run into:

1. Early Decision
2. Early Decision 2
3. Restrictive Early Action
4. Early Action
5. Regular Decision
6. Rolling Admission

These six admissions plans fall into two categories:

- Restrictive: There are rules about applying to other schools at the same time. Think of this like being in an exclusive relationship. You can't date other colleges.

- Non-restrictive: There are no rules about applying to other schools at the same time. You can date other colleges. Woo hoo!

Let's break down the various admissions plans. We will start with the three restrictive ones: Early Decision, Early Decision 2, and Restrictive Early Action.

Early Decision (ED)/Early Decision 2 (ED2)	
Category	Restrictive
Summary	You can only apply ED to one college; if you are accepted, you must attend that school. ED2 works exactly the same way but has a later timeline.
Timeline	**ED** Deadline: between mid-October and mid-December Notification: between late December and early February **ED 2** Deadline: sometime in January Notification: sometime in February

Recommended if:	• You're certain the school is your first choice. • You have good reason to believe you can get in. • Your application components are strong and polished. • You're sure you can afford this school (if you have financial need). • You want to be considered for certain school-specific scholarships. • You're looking for an edge; applying ED shows strong interest.

Restrictive Early Action (REA) *also known as Single-Choice Early Action*	
Category	Restrictive
Summary	As with ED, you can only apply REA to one school; unlike ED, however, acceptance under REA is not binding.
Timeline	Deadline: between mid-October and mid-December Notification: between late December and early February
Recommended if:	• You're certain the school is a great fit. • You have good reason to believe you can get in. • Your application components are strong and polished. • You're sure you can afford this school (if you have financial need). • You want to be considered for certain school-specific scholarships. • You're looking for an edge; applying REA shows strong interest.

Now let's move onto the three non-restrictive admissions plans: Early Action, Regular Decision, and Rolling Admission. Remember, "non-restrictive" means there are no rules about applying to other colleges at the same time.

Early Action (EA)	
Category	Non-restrictive
Summary	You can apply EA to as many schools as you would like; if you are accepted under the EA plan, the decision is not binding.
Timeline	Deadline: between mid-October and mid-December Notification: between late December and early February

Recommended if:	• You've thoroughly researched and feel confident about the school. • You have good reason to believe you can get in. • Your application components are strong and polished. • You want to be considered for certain school-specific scholarships.

Regular Decision (RD)	
Category	Non-restrictive
Summary	You can apply EA to as many schools as you would like; if you are accepted under the EA plan, the decision is not binding.
Timeline	Deadline: between mid-October and mid-December Notification: between late December and early February
Recommended if:	• You need the fall semester to strengthen your application components. • You need the fall semester to improve your GPA and/or test scores. • You need more time to weigh college and financial aid options.

Rolling Admission (RA)	
Category	Non-restrictive
Summary	You can apply to as many schools with RA as you'd like; students are accepted on a first-come, first-served basis. Though there is no stated deadline, there are limited spots which get filled as applications roll in.
Timeline	"Rolls" all year; however, some colleges may require you to apply by a certain deadline to be considered for school-specific scholarships.
Recommended if:	Schools you're interested in have a Rolling Admissions plan.

I have good news! You aren't going to pick colleges based on the admissions plans they offer. You will apply to schools that are a good fit for you, and then you will select from among the admissions plans they offer. All of the above boils down to this:

• You can apply to college during the fall or spring semester of senior year.

• Some admissions plans bind you to acceptance, while others don't.

- Some admissions plans have rules about applying to other schools simultaneously, while others don't.

Once you know which colleges you will apply to, use the information in this section to select the admissions plan that makes most sense for you. And, as always, pay close attention to each college's unique requirements and deadlines!

Tell Your Whole Story

In a holistic admissions process, colleges are interested not only in your grades and test scores but also the qualitative components—essays, recommendation letters, etc.—which paint a fuller picture of who you are. Admissions officers are left to make the best decisions they can with the information you give them. The question is: will you provide all the information they need to evaluate you fairly?

In August 2016, a flood <u>ravaged</u> my home city, Baton Rouge, and much of southeast Louisiana. Dozens of students and their families lost <u>virtually</u> everything and had to stay in hotels or with relatives. Many of these students understandably experienced a dip in their grades as they focused less on school and more on survival. In their college applications, we made sure to explain these circumstances. It was important for colleges to realize that the drop in academic performance was not because of laziness but a natural disaster.

Your circumstances don't have to be <u>dire</u> to justify explaining them. Imagine that, during both 9th and 10th grade, you played varsity soccer, wrote for the newspaper, and served on student government, but after 10th grade, you <u>abruptly</u> stopped all extracurricular activities. It wasn't because you were a quitter. Rather, your parents asked you to start watching your younger siblings each day after school. Without an explanation, colleges might wonder why you dropped your commitments.

Holistic admissions exist so you can tell your whole story. If something took place that may hurt your admissions chances but does not reflect your ability or potential, explain it. Let's talk about how.

Ways to Tell Your Whole Story

- **Essays**: Your personal statement and/or writing supplements are great chances to shine a light on challenging circumstances.

- **"Additional information" section:** Most applications have this optional section, which is a perfect place to explain special circumstances. See example on next page.

- **Admissions interview:** This is usually not mandatory, but if you have special circumstances to explain, an interview is a great chance to <u>self-advocate</u>.

Example
Additional Information
Please attach a separate sheet if you wish to provide details of circumstances or qualifications not reflected in the application. *(This is the exact wording from The Common Application).*

Dear Admissions Committee:

You will notice that the big drop in my grades during my spring sophomore semester is inconsistent with my overall academic performance. In January 2012 my family and I were evicted from our home and spent the next four months living in a variety of places. Sometimes we stayed with friends, sometimes at a local shelter, and sometimes at our church. During this period, I missed many days of school. My parents lacked reliable transportation and the bus could not predict where to pick me up. Worrying about my family—and especially my younger siblings—made focusing on school difficult, and my living situation was not always helpful for completing schoolwork. Thankfully, my mom and I both got jobs at the end of the semester, and that enabled my family to secure a home where we have been living ever since. And as you can see in my transcript, our new environment has been suitable for me to earn the kinds of grades I am capable of earning. I appreciate you giving me the chance to explain my situation, and I promise that if I have the chance to attend University of Washington, a dip like this will not occur again. Thank you.

Help Your Counselor Help You

You can't apply to college without your high school counselor, so it's important to know how to make it easy for this person to help you. Your counselor will appreciate your effort to make their life just a little less stressful.

Depending on the college, you may need all of the following from your counselor:

- Official high school transcript (always required)
- School report (usually required)
- Counselor recommendation (usually optional; depends how well they know you)
- Fee waiver (if you are financially eligible)

When to ask

Remember that your counselor is helping many other students. Set yourself and your counselor up for success by requesting anything you need at least six weeks in advance of any deadline. Give him or her plenty of time to get the job done.

How to ask

Step 1: Get organized

Before you talk to your counselor, prep the following:

- Résumé – If your counselor has to write a recommendation letter for you, having an updated résumé will help a lot, especially if they doesn't know you well.
- Requirements and due dates – Most students won't do this, but you can. Create a document outlining what each of your colleges requires from your counselor. Here is how you could set it up to make it nice and easy:

College *Which college?*	Address *What's the admissions office address?*	Requirements *What's needed from the counselor?*	Deadline *When is everything due?*	Submission *How should the counselor submit?*
Colby College	Office of Admissions Colby College 4800 Mayflower HIll Waterville, ME 04901	• Counselor Recommendation letter • Official transcript • School report	11/15/19	Common Application (online)

Step 2: Arrange a time to drop off your materials

Email your counselor to request a meeting to review where you are applying and what you need from her or him. Here's an example of an email you could send:

> Dear (counselor's name),
>
> I was wondering if I could drop by one day this week for a few minutes to discuss the colleges I am applying to and each one's different requirements. I know you are extremely busy, which is why I have organized my materials to make it as easy as possible for you to help me. Please let me know if there is a particular day or time when you would prefer for me to visit. Thanks so much.
>
> Sincerely,
>
> (your name)

Step 3: Invite your counselor

Whether you're applying through the Common App or another platform, you will have to "invite" your counselor to begin submitting materials required for your application. You will have to enter your counselor's name and contact information, and then they should receive an automated email explaining the next steps.

Step 4: Follow up

Make no mistake: while it is your counselor's job to submit your materials, it is *your* job to make sure they actually do it. In your online application portal, you can usually see whether your counselor has submitted the required materials. If they haven't, and the deadline is approaching, it is appropriate to gently nudge your counselor by emailing or popping in their office. Just be polite and understanding when you do it.

Step 5: Send a thank-you note

Unlike picking your nose and eating your boogers, showing gratitude is a good habit. Once your applications are complete, write your counselor a handwritten note to express your thanks. Finally, it's nice to let your counselor know when you hear back from the schools you applied to.

Sample thank-you note to counselor

Dear (counselor's name),

I really appreciate all the time and energy you took to send my materials to all of my colleges. I know you are very busy, and I do not take your help or time for granted. As I receive decision letters from colleges, I will be sure to let you know. Thanks so much again for all that you do!

Sincerely,

(your name)

Don't Post That!

Ask your grandma to Google you. If she doesn't like what she sees, you may have a problem.

By now you know that some colleges will go the extra mile to learn more about you. This includes looking into your activity on Instagram, Snapchat, Facebook, and other social media platforms.

Don't believe me? A 2014 Kaplan Test Prep poll of over 400 college admissions officers revealed that 35% (more than one in every three) had visited an applicant's social media profile to learn more about them. When Kaplan did the same poll in 2008, fewer than 10% of admissions officers reported having done so. Use of social media as a factor in college admissions seems to be trending ...up.

Your social media presence likely won't help you in the college admissions process, but it *can* hurt you. I would advise against posts or comments connected to any of the following, and you might consider striking a few of these from your life altogether:

- Alcohol
- Drugs
- Other <u>illicit</u>/banned substances
- Profanity
- Sexual activity
- Criminal activity
- Discriminatory and insensitive comments
- Anything calling your character, judgment, or morality into question

I'm not saying to <u>rid</u> your social media presence of all personality. Do you! Just be mindful not to post anything that could cause a college admissions officer to wonder if you would be a <u>liability</u> instead of an <u>asset</u> to their campus.

You're smart enough to know the difference, but if you need a second opinion, ask a peer or adult with solid judgment. Or, go ask Grandma.

What You Need to Know About Recommendation Letters

What is a recommendation letter?

A letter in which a teacher, coach, boss, or mentor shares nice things about you and recommends you for acceptance to the college(s) you are applying to.

When it comes to recommendation letters, do all colleges have the same requirements?

Of course not! That would be too easy. Some colleges don't require them at all. For the colleges that do, you need to pay attention to each school's unique requirements.

How important are recommendation letters?

For colleges that require them, they're crucial. Remember that rec letters are one of the Big Five.

What makes a recommendation letter <u>effective</u>?

The best recommendation letters are:

- Personalized - the letter could not possibly be about another student.
- Detailed - recommender gives plenty of examples to prove you are great.
- Illuminating - recommender shares info not found in the rest of your application.

What makes a recommendation letter <u>ineffective</u>?

Ineffective recommendation letters are the <u>inverse</u> of above. They are:

- Cookie-cutter - the letter could be about anyone.
- All talk - recommender gives no examples to prove you are great.
- <u>Redundant</u> - recommender repeats info found elsewhere in your application.

Who can write my recommendation letter?

You always need to pay close attention to each college's unique recommendation letter requirements. However, here are some guidelines:

- Choose 1–2 core subject teachers—math, English, social studies, science, or foreign language—from 11th or 12th grade only.

- Choose teachers who have good things to say about you and who know you well as both a student and a person.

- Some schools offer the option to submit additional letters from non-core teachers or non-academic adults (e.g., coach, boss, mentor, etc.). If you have this option and possess solid relationships with these types of people, I urge you to request recommendation letters from them. These unique perspectives can strengthen your application significantly.

- If possible choose recommenders who have plenty of experience working with youth. Colleges value their perspectives. It's nice to have, but don't stress about this.

Is there anyone who should not write my recommendation letter?

Unless one of your colleges expressly requests it, do not ask friends or family members for recommendation letters.

How to Secure Recommendation Letters

No matter how much your recommenders love you, you are adding work to their plates by requesting letters. They already work full-time and, in the case of teachers, are likely writing letters for other students. Remember, how strong your recommenders' letters are will impact your chances of getting into college. Your job is to make it easy as possible for your recommenders to help you. Let's talk about how.

When to ask

You should request letters of recommendation at least one month in advance of any college's deadline.

How to ask

Step 1: Get organized - Before you ask, prepare the following:

- Résumé – Use the worksheets I've provided in chapter 2 to record important information about your high school career and future plans. Even for recommenders who know you well, having this information makes life easier.

- Requirements and due dates – Know each college's application deadline.

Step 2: Make the ask(s)

Send a formal email to each recommender. Below is a sample. It should work in most situations, but **please personalize it**! You want personalized recommendation letters; the least you can do is request them in a personalized way. Don't forget to attach your updated résumé.

Sample email to request a recommendation letter

Dear (recommender's name),

I hope this finds you well.

I am in the process of applying to college and am writing, with gratitude, to ask you to serve as one of my recommenders. I believe you would do an excellent job describing what I can bring to a college in and out of the classroom, and I would be honored for you to recommend me.

I know how busy you are, which is why I want to make this process as easy for you as possible. First, I have attached my résumé, which gives a snapshot of my academic and non-academic life as well as my future plans.

I would also like to share the application deadlines for each of my colleges:

- College #1 – Deadline
- College #2 – Deadline
- College #3 – Deadline
- College #4 – Deadline

Let me know if there is any other information that would help you in this process. If you accept my request, I will sign you up to be my recommender, and you should then receive an email with instructions about next steps.

Thank you for your consideration and all you have done to support me during high school, and I look forward to hearing from you when it is convenient.

Sincerely,

(your name)

Step 3: Invite your recommenders

Whether you're applying through the Common App or another platform, you will have to "invite" your recommenders to submit their letters. As you did with your counselor, you will enter your recommenders' names and contact information, and then they should receive automated emails explaining next steps.

Step 4: Follow up

It's your job to stay on your recommenders to ensure letters get submitted on time. In your online application portal, you can usually see if a recommender has submitted their letter. If they haven't and the deadline is approaching, it's okay to gently nudge your recommender with an email or phone call. Just be polite and understanding.

Step 5: Send a thank-you note

Unlike biting your toenails, showing gratitude is a good habit. Once your applications are complete, write each recommender a handwritten note or email to express your thanks. Finally, it's nice to let your recommenders' know when you hear back from the schools you applied to.

Tips for All College Essays

During the college application process, you are likely to encounter many different essay assignments of varying topics and lengths. I've seen them all, and I've found that the ten writing tips below are essential no matter the situation. The first five tips focus on content and the second five on style.

Content Tips: What You Write

1. Make one point and stick to it

No matter your essay's length, your objective is to prove a single point. Your point should be clear and easy to follow. Imagine your essay is a beaded necklace. The beads represent the various pieces of evidence, reflection, and analysis you will use to develop your point. The string is your point. There is only one, it is there throughout, and it holds everything together.

2. Make your essay personal

Personal means about you. The opposite of personal is impersonal: fact-based and emotionally detached.

Impersonal vs. personal writing

Impersonal: Cigarettes are extremely unhealthy. Each year thousands of people die of lung cancer brought on by smoking.

Personal: Last October, I lost my Aunt Ilene to lung cancer. Even more than the Surgeon General's warning, her death is a constant reminder of the fact that smoking can ruin a person's life.

There are two reasons to make your essays personal. First, these essays are for colleges to get to know you. Regardless of the topic, your essay should be a story about you. Second, your essay needs to be interesting. The admissions officer reading your essay will almost certainly be a human, and humans enjoy reading about other humans.

3. Don't be all talk

When you write a college essay, you are a lawyer. Your job is to make one argument and prove it's true. To do that, you must provide evidence—experiences, examples, facts, details, etc.—as well as reflection and analysis to back up your point. Here's an example:

Example of providing evidence

When I was younger, all that my dad said was doctrine and anything he did I, naturally, copied. We played rocket ship games in the pool, stayed up too late reading bedtime stories and ran through the corn mazes at Terhune's Orchard. In second grade, I broke my wrist running toward my dad and never would have guessed that, just a few years later, I would sprain my ankle running away from him.

As I grew older, he was no longer as cool as he used to be. He became the enemy—a total embarrassment. He wore his socks too high and whistled too loudly. He listened to horrific country music while carpooling six other 12-year-old girls to soccer games. In front of my friends, his bold laugh paralyzed me.

This is an excerpt from an essay about a girl's changing relationship with her father as she grows up. Notice how she uses several concrete examples to support the opening sentence of each paragraph.

In addition to providing evidence, you should also reflect on and analyze your evidence. In a college essay, this means occasionally zooming out to share your thoughts and feelings. This commentary develops your evidence and strengthens your one main argument. This concept is slightly harder to explain, so I am going to use a different excerpt from the same essay to illustrate my point.

Example of reflecting and analyzing the evidence

However, the catastrophes that occurred in school were by far the worst. On Halloween, in seventh grade, my class went outside to watch the Lower School Halloween parade. To my surprise, my father had dressed up as Chewbacca from Star Wars, sound effects included, and was leading the march around the school. In fifth grade he, the only father, came to our Girl Scout retreat, guitar in hand, and made up songs (which in hindsight seems propagandistic) like, "Boys are stupid, boys are dumb, boys just don't know how to have fun!" Just kill me. **Every time he spoke I wanted to crawl away. He invaded my privacy, humiliated me in front of my friends and seemed to be the least cool parent ever.**

As you can see from her opening line, this paragraph continues to develop the point that it took a very long time before the writer saw her dad as anything but embarrassing. I have bolded the last few sentences to show an example of analyzing the evidence. Unlike in the rest of the paragraph, in the bolded portion the writer takes a break from explaining what happened to tell you what she thought and felt about it. This commentary does two things for your essay. First, it strengthens the evidence by linking it back to the main argument. Second, it lets the reader inside the mind and heart of the writer, making the essay more personal.

4. Avoid clichéd language

Avoid well-known sayings, like the ones listed below, to express your thoughts.

- It is what it is
- Come full circle
- For all intents and purposes
- When all is said and done
- At the end of the day

Instead, just write what you mean to say using your own words.

Similarly, avoid famous quotes or song lyrics as substitutes for your own thoughts. If you use a quote in your essay, make sure you analyze the quote and explain why you've included it. That includes biblical quotes.

Ineffective vs. effective use of a quote

Ineffective: In conclusion, when it comes to my dreams and aspirations, it's like Notorious B.I.G. said: "The sky's the limit." (Song lyric substitutes writer's own thoughts.)

Effective: Junior year, I began listening to Childish Gambino. His songs said what I wanted to: "I'm sorry man, but I act me; I don't act 'black,' whatever that be." I recognize it is cheesy to cite a song lyric as my inspiration, but I'm just being honest. It made me realize I let others' views define me, and thus my isolation was partially self-inflicted." (Writer uses song lyrics to develop his point.)

---

5. Make sure your essay is error-free

Errors include:

- Spelling, punctuation, and grammatical mistakes
- Misused words (words that don't mean what you think they do)
- Run-on sentences
- Factually incorrect information
- Referring to the wrong college (if your essay talks about the college)

Style Tips: How You Write

1. Open strong

A strong opening line grabs the reader, making her want to continue reading. Below are some examples of opening lines that worked.

Opening lines that worked

- I waited for a stranger, my dad, to pick me up at the airport.
- When I was in eighth grade, I couldn't read.
- I have old hands.
- I have been surfing Lake Michigan since I was 3 years old.
- I change my name each time I place an order at Starbucks.
- As an American-Indian, I am forever bound to the hyphen.
- Her eighty-year-old fingers felt like frozen fish sticks on my cheek.

Note: your opening line does not have to be shocking, just interesting.

2. Write descriptively

Vague, non-descriptive language is boring and makes it hard for your reader to connect with your experience. Descriptive language brings your story to life.

Descriptive vs. non-descriptive writing

Example 1: about acting in a play

Non-descriptive: As I prepared to walk on stage, I became more and more nervous.

Descriptive: As showtime approached, I grew nervous to the point of nausea, my heart slamming against my ribcage like it was trying to escape my body.

Example 2: about a girl making candy with her mom

Non-descriptive: I stirred the mix for a long time and, when it was ready, my mother poured it into a pan.

Descriptive: Ninety minutes of non-stop stirring turned the sugary broth into a chunky, gooey goop, which she poured into an old rectangular pan that had seen better days.

---

3. Write leanly

Lean means concise, or fewer words. Always cut words you don't need. Lean writing is more effective than wordy, fluffy writing.

Unnecessary words distract the reader from your point. Think of your essay like a piece of meat: cut the fat.

Example of lean writing

Example 1

Original Version: In Biology class, we work collaboratively on unfamiliar and open-ended problems.

Leaner Version: In Biology class, we collaborated on unfamiliar, open-ended problems.

Example 2

Original Version: The teacher discussed several ways that participation in after-school programs is important during his speech to the class.

Leaner Version: In his speech to the class, the teacher discussed the importance of participation in after-school programs.

---

4. Write simply and clearly

This goes hand in hand with Style Tip #3. Don't complicate sentences to seem smart. It will be obvious that you're trying too hard. Don't use "big words" to prove you know them; use them to enhance sentences. Simple, clear writing shows confidence, maturity, and humility. Your reader will love you for it.

Overly complicated vs. simple, clear writing

Overly complicated: By age ten, my extraordinarily passionate love affair with the sport of football transcended what by conventional standards would be considered normal for a boy that age, and this could be seen in the fact that I was spending as much time on a football field as members of my school's high school varsity team.

Simple, clear: By age ten, I was spending as much time on a football field as members of my school's varsity team.

Simple, clear writing packs greater meaning into fewer words. This is particularly important with college essays, in which you have to share a lot but also stay within the prescribed word count.

5. Write in first person

A college essay is not an academic paper. College admissions officers want to hear about you from you. Writing in the first person will make it sound like you're talking to the reader, making your essay more personal.

First person pronouns: I, we, me, us, my, mine, our, ours

First person vs. third person

Third person: Different people have different relationships with their grandparents, and those different relationships are based on different things. Sometimes grandparents and their grandkids bond over sports or movies, and sometimes over a shared love of baking.

First person: My grandmother taught me how to bake when I was four. With my hands straight up in the air, my fingertips barely reached the height of the kitchen counter, so her first step was getting me a stool. I keep that stool in my room as a reminder of my grandmother and the love of baking which she imparted to me.

How to Write a Great Personal Statement

A personal statement is simply an essay. When required, it's a crucial part of your college application—one of our Big Five.

An effective personal statement is well-written and <u>reveals</u> important information about your history, personality, character, and goals. The key word is "reveals." Your personal statement should open a window into your life you might usually keep shut. In that respect, this process takes courage.

Let's talk about how to write the kind of personal statement that tips the scales in your favor.

Brainstorm: deciding what to write about

A "prompt" is a question or statement that your personal statement should address. Let's look at two examples of personal statement prompts:

Prompt 1: *Describe the world you come from—for example, your family, community or school – and tell us how your world has shaped your dreams and aspirations.*

Prompt 2: *Some students have a background, identity, interest, or talent that is so meaningful they believe their application would be incomplete without it. If this sounds like you, then please share your story.*

Step 1: Simplify the prompt

I don't know about you, but these prompts make my brain feel like mush. They are so broad and open-ended. Where do you begin? First, reword and simplify the prompt so it's easier to wrap your head around. Let's do that with the two prompts above:

Prompt 1 reworded and simplified: *Write about one part of your life that has made you who you are. It could be your family, community, school, sports team, or something else. In what ways has this one part of your life affected your future plans?*

Prompt 2 reworded and simplified: *Tell us something about yourself we must know in order to really get you. It can be a story, a moment, an interest, a talent—pretty much anything.*

Step 2: Narrow the prompt

Personal statement prompts are intentionally broad so students have lots of choices and flexibility. Let's narrow Prompt 1 and see how it helps us to focus.

Prompt 1 reworded and simplified: *Write about one part of your life that has made you who you are. It could be your family, community, school, sports team, or something else. In what ways has this one part of your life affected your future plans?*

Prompt 1 reworded, simplified, and narrowed: *Tell us about your family. How have your experiences with your family influenced your goals and future plans?*

Step 3: Make connections, part 1

Now that your prompt is easier to digest, it's time make connections between the current focus of your essay and other aspects of your life. Take out a sheet of paper and go to a place where you can think clearly and creatively.

In the center of your sheet, write whatever word is currently the focus of your essay. I'm going to write "family." This next part is key.

Jot down the people, experiences, objects, and places you connect with your focus. Think deeply. Make literal as well as figurative connections. For example, under objects I might write "tie" because my dad always wears one. That's a literal connection, but what does the tie make me think and feel on a deeper level? Maybe ties make me think of my dad rarely being home because he's always working. Maybe that makes me sad. That's a figurative connection.

When a person, experience, object, or place connects you to deeper thoughts and emotions, write them down. Flesh those connections all the way out. For instance:

| Ties | → | Dad always wears a tie | → | Dad's always dressed for work | → | Dad's rarely home | → | Sadness |

Don't hold back. Write everything that comes into your head. If you need a paper for every category, go for it. When you feel you've maxed out, stop and take a break.

Cut your people, experiences, objects, and places down to the most important 10—not 10 in each category but total. Then cut them to 5, then 3, then 1. Continuing with our example, let's say my most significant item is "Dad," my most <u>salient</u> connection to my family.

Step 4: Make connections, part 2

My new focus is "Dad." Once again, I can narrow the prompt. Just for fun, let's look at how our prompt has evolved from the beginning.

Original: *Describe the world you come from – for example, your family, community or school – and tell us how your world has shaped your dreams and aspirations.*

Reworded and simplified: *Write about one part of your life that has made you who you are. It could be your family, community, school, sports team, or something else. In what ways has this one part of your life affected your future plans?*

Reworded, simplified, and narrowed: *Tell us about your family. How have your experiences with your family influenced your goals and future plans?*

Specific topic: *Tell us about your relationship with your dad. How has your relationship with your dad influenced your goals and future plans?*

Our new prompt is still in line with the original. We've just made it easier to understand and to stay focused on.

Take out a new brainstorming sheet, writing your new focus in the middle. Remember, mine is "Dad." Conduct another brainstorm, connecting your new focus to people, experiences, objects, and places in your life. You may be able to pull some of these connections from the first time we did this exercise.

Flesh out each item thoroughly! What does each make you feel, think, remember, smell? The harder you work on this section, the easier your final product will be to write.

Examples

People

- Grandpa—was an engineer like Dad; worked a ton; thinks in numbers
- Students—felt like he cared about them more than me

Experiences

- 9th birthday—Dad had to miss it because he was working
- Science fair—Dad showed up but was disappointed I didn't win

Objects

- Tie—reminds me of Dad always working and me missing him
- Coffee—smell woke me up; reminds me of Dad getting up early to work

Places

- Treehouse—Dad and I built it together; was a bonding experience
- Home office—door always closed; I was too scared to go in

Step 5: Draft your one main point

Every college essay needs one main point you will spend your essay proving. Take a long, hard look at the prompt and your most recent brainstorming sheet. Write a summarizing statement in a few sentences. Here's an example:

> *My relationship with my dad has defined who I am and want to be, personally and professionally. As a professional, my dad is my example. His career has inspired me to reach similar and greater heights in the field of mechanical engineering. As a dad, though, he is my non-example. Until further notice, he is the sort of father I will strive never to be for my own children.*

Your summary doesn't need to be perfectly written, just simple and real. If you've done a good job, you've written your essay's main point, the argument you will spend your essay proving. And if you've done a good job brainstorming, you've got the proof—the specific details you will use throughout the essay to support your argument.

A final note on brainstorming

I have done my best to turn brainstorming into a clear, step-by-step process, but it may not work for you. If you find yourself stuck and uninspired, here are some questions that may help you reveal the stuff of great personal statements.

Brainstorming Questions

1. What do people not know about you?
2. What thought causes you the most pain? The most joy?
3. What experience caused you the most pain? The most joy?
4. How are you different when no one's watching?
5. What's the most beautiful place in the world?
6. When you're happiest, what are you doing, who are you with, and where are you?
7. When do you feel like the best version of yourself? When do you not?
8. What are you most afraid of?
9. What smells bring you back in time?
10. When did you fail miserably?
11. What have you not told the people closest to you?
12. What has your dad taught you? What about your mom?

13. What are you sensitive about?

14. Who knows you so well it makes you uncomfortable?

15. Who knows things about you that you wish they didn't? What do they know?

16. What's a memory you couldn't forget if you tried?

17. What or who are you waiting for?

18. What is your greatest strength? Greatest weakness?

19. What wouldn't you trade for the world?

20. What do you love to learn about? Talk about?

21. Which inanimate items in your life matter to you most?

22. Who would you risk your life for?

23. Who counts on you? And for what?

24. What will they say about you when you're gone?

25. What's missing?

Structure - Organizing Your Essay

There are myriad ways to structure a personal statement. I'm going to focus on two:

A great personal statement or other college essay should either go deep or wide as you work to prove your one main point.

- **Deep:** proving your one main point by sharing, in great detail, 1–2 critically important scenes or experiences from your life.

- **Wide:** proving your one main point by discussing many different experiences or pieces of your life.

For examples of deep and wide personal statements, check out "Essays That Worked" later in this chapter.

Approach 1: Going Deep

A "deep" essay shares one or a few experiences in graphic detail. What makes it a "narrative" is that events take place chronologically and are linked causally—meaning one event affects the next, and so on, like dominoes.

Many movies "go deep" to prove their point. A good example is *Saving Private Ryan*. Just as the example above was broadly about my family, *Saving Private Ryan* is broadly about World War II. Just as I decided to talk about my family through the lens of my relationship with my dad, *Saving Private Ryan* portrays the terror of WWII through the lens of one particular story. The movie gives us a deep narrative.

Saving Private Ryan follows a platoon of soldiers, led by Captain John Miller, who have a special mission to go behind enemy lines, find Private James Ryan, and bring him back to the U.S. safely. We learn early in the movie that Private Ryan's three brothers have all been killed in the war. Captain Miller and his men will carry out what is basically a suicide mission to save Private Ryan and spare his mother the horror of losing all four of her sons in the war.

The <u>scope</u> of WWII is beyond our comprehension. It would be impossible to tell the whole story of the war in one movie or a hundred. Recognizing this, director Steven Spielberg chooses instead to "go deep," inserting us into one narrative about one group of soldiers. Occasionally, he zooms out from the action to give us a sense of the war's massive global scale or to allow us to reflect on what the characters are going through. For the most part, though, he remains zoomed in on these men—their battles, friendships, fears, dreams, and for some, deaths. Through this one intimate, personal story, we can better understand WWII's total, <u>unfathomable</u> devastation.

Like WWII, your life story cannot easily be summed up. So, like Spielberg, you can "go deep," sharing in vivid detail one or two narratives that illustrate your main point. At points in your story, you will zoom out to share analysis and reflection or provide a sense of the larger backdrop against which your scenes are set. For the most part, though, you are zoomed in on 1–2 critical experiences. Your reader will use what you give them to fill in the blanks.

"Saving Private Ryan" is one of thousands of films that "go deep" to make a broader point, but it provides a nice blueprint for structuring a deep, narrative personal statement. There are many approaches. What I am offering here are just guidelines.

Structure of a "Going Deep" Personal Statement *Saving Private Ryan* vs. Your Essay		
Element	*Saving Private Ryan*	**Your Essay**
Main point	WWII was devastating, not only in its global impact but in its effect on the lives of soldiers and families directly involved with the war.	The goal of your essay is to prove one point. You may never explicitly state it, but you spend your essay proving it using evidence (i.e., concrete details and examples).
Opening statement	The movie opens in Arlington National Cemetery in Washington, D.C., a burial ground for U.S. soldiers. A character we don't know stops at a grave. Then we are taken back in time to the brutal scene of D-Day, the storming of the beaches of Normandy in France. We don't quite know how the story will unfold, but we're hooked.	When you "go deep," hook your reader with a compelling opening line and thrust her or him into your scene. You don't need to provide background information yet. Just get the reader invested.
Context— introduce the main point or problem	We get some background info so we under-stand the story. We learn that Private James Ryan's three brothers have been killed. The movie is going to be about Captain John Miller's platoon trying to rescue him. Now we know why the film is called "Saving Private Ryan."	Provide some background information so the reader is not lost. This is where you will show the reader the main point you will be proving.
Body—tell your story	The film follows Captain Ryan's men as they try to find and rescue Private Ryan. We watch the soldiers fight, but we get to know them between battles. Now and then, the film zooms out to give us a big-picture view of the war.	Illustrate your main point by sharing one or a few scenes in great detail. Along the way, zoom out to share reflection, analysis, or background info. Mainly, though, you should stay zoomed in.
Conclusion— reflection and resolution	We learn Private Ryan is on his way home to his mom. The film brings us back to the opening scene. The character we didn't know is a much older version of Private Ryan. He's with his whole family, grandkids and all. He stands at the tomb of Captain Miller, his rescuer. Ryan thanks Miller for having saved him and wonders if his life was worth those of the men who fought to save him. The film ends with Private Ryan saluting his fallen captain. We see Ryan's large, beautiful family standing behind him, a reminder that the sacrifice had been worth it.	End your story with some closure, a resolution to the main problem. Share your reflections. Discuss what you learned from the experience. Give the reader a sense of what happens next, where the characters go from here. You don't have to take the reader back to your opening scene, but it is effective to round out the essay by calling on things you said earlier in the piece.

Approach 2: Going Wide

There are two ways to "go wide."

First is a wide narrative. Remember, "narrative" simply means events take place chronologically and are linked causally. While a "deep" narrative looks at one or two scenes in great detail, a wide narrative covers a long period of time. This approach works well for personal statements showing gradual change over many years, like a biographical essay (the QuestBridge Scholarship asks for this).

An example of this is the film *Boyhood*, a coming-of-age story depicting a boy's youth from ages six to eighteen as he grows up in Texas with divorced parents. *Boyhood* made headlines because it was shot over 12 years, showing the actual aging of the main characters. The film does not last 12 years. It's a two-hour narrative comprised of a selection of key experiences spanning that timeframe. We don't see every moment of the main character's life, but from the scenes we do see, we get a fairly complete picture and fill in the blanks as needed.

For a wide narrative, the same fundamentals of college essay writing apply (see "Tips for All College Essays.") Like a deep narrative, a wide narrative must have one main point or theme holding it together. Descriptive and specific language are equally important. The biggest difference between a deep and wide narrative is in the amount of time each sentence moves the reader forward. In a deep narrative, a sentence may advance the reader a few seconds; in a wide one, a sentence could equal months or years.

The structure of a wide narrative can be similar to that of a deep narrative. The opening sentence and intro should still hook the reader. Following that should be some context, and the concluding paragraph should mainly be resolution and reflection. The difference will be in the body, where you will cover more events in less granular detail.

A second way to "go wide" is to write a montage essay, where you discuss various elements in your life and connect them with one theme. A montage is not a narrative, meaning the events or elements have no causal relationship.

The montage style can be seen in the documentary film *Babies*, which follows four children—in Namibia, Mongolia, Japan, and San Francisco—during their first year of life. With no narration, the film jumps from baby to baby for 79 minutes, comparing the cultural differences in each setting.

A montage essay depends on three big components: theme, lens, and elements. "Theme" is the broad topic your essay is about. In *Babies*, the theme is cultural differences. Since the theme can be very broad, we need a lens to focus it. In *Babies*, the lens is, well, babies. "Elements" are pieces of evidence that illustrate the theme. In *Babies*, there are countless elements—food, dress, traditions, and more—that show cultural differences between the babies and their families.

Montage essays are cool because they let you pull together aspects of your life that seem disconnected. The brainstorming exercise a few pages back will help you generate a list of these aspects, or elements. Just make sure you have a theme (a broad idea everything comes back to) and a lens (a way to focus your theme). If you don't, your essay will be disjointed.

I wish you happy writing! And, I urge you to read "Essays That Worked" so you can see my advice in action.

Write a Great "Why Us" Essay

Many colleges will ask you to write an essay that addresses this question: why are you interested in our school? In other words: why us? Let's talk about how to tackle this question.

Think of your favorite restaurant. Imagine I asked you to write an essay telling me why you want to eat there. Give me four reasons, one word each. Write them down.

Here's what I would put:

- Food
- Health
- Service
- Environment

Now, <u>expound</u> upon each one-word response with a short, personalized explanation. Make each one about you. Here's an example:

- It offers my favorite type of food.
- The food is not only good but healthy, which I care about.
- Waiters check in often, which is good because I drink a lot of water.
- The relaxing environment calms me down after a rough day.

Even a restaurant with great reviews may not be your favorite. For one to be your favorite, it must meet your unique needs and wants. If you were to write an essay explaining why you want to eat there, you would really be writing about yourself—about how the restaurant meets what you are specifically looking for in a dining experience.

It's the same idea with the "why us?" essay. You're really writing about you—the specific ways this college matches your personality, values, needs, and wants.

There's one catch. Colleges want you to want them. You need to prove you understand what makes each one <u>unique</u>. This makes admissions officers feel warm and fuzzy and, more importantly, shows your legitimate passion for the school.

The "why us?" question comes down to two tasks:

Primary task: Discuss the ways the college matches what you are looking for.

Secondary task: Prove you know what makes this college special.

Before we begin the outlining process, I have to tell you two things:

1. **Research:** You can't write a strong "why us?" essay without doing solid research. If you don't know much about the school, it will be obvious.

2. **Fake it 'til you make it:** You may not be writing about your first-choice school. In fact, you may have little interest in the school. Fake it. Get the job done.

Outlining Your "Why Us?" Essay
Step One: Determine your "match points"

A "match point" is a specific feature of the college that you value and makes the school a match for you. Focus on 3–4. Below is a list of possible match points. These will get you thinking, but they are written generally. Yours must be specific to the college. It's possible that out of your 3–4 match points, there's a top one. It's okay if that one takes up more space than the others.

Examples of Match Points

- The college's academic philosophy or values
- Type of curriculum the college uses
- Focus on diversity and inclusion
- A particular major or academic program
- Research opportunities with professors
- A focus on collaborative learning
- Supportive faculty and school staff
- A special non-academic program that is offered
- School culture/campus experience
- Opportunities for community service in the surrounding area
- Track record of graduates succeeding in a certain professional field

Below are examples of what a match point is *not*. It's okay if you mention them in your essay, but they should not be your focus:

- Your parents went there
- You grew up thinking you'd go there
- Campus
- Weather
- Sports (unless you're an athlete)
- Food
- Dorms
- Party scene

Step Two: State why each match point is important to you

Write a statement explaining why each of your 3–4 match points is particularly important to you. These will serve as the topic sentences or opening lines of your body paragraphs. A "why statement" doesn't have to be just one sentence.

Example "why statements" for Junction College (fake school)

Match point 1: the teacher training program

Why statement 1: Education has been my portal to a better life, which is why I have always dreamed of being a teacher—a role that will allow me to support students the way so many teachers have supported me. Junction College's secondary education program is the ideal vehicle to pursue this long-held goal.

Match point 2: focus on diversity

Why statement 2: My experience has been that the deepest, longest-lasting learning happens when I consider the perspectives of people from backgrounds different from my own. What excites me most about Junction College is its focus on diversity as a tool for educating its students.

Step Three: Support your "why statements"

As with any college essay, you are trying to prove one point: that you sincerely want to attend this college. You need to prove your point with evidence.

For each statement, write 3–5 supporting details that illustrate the specific ways the match point comes to life at the college.

Your supporting details must be specific. This shows that you have researched the school and understand what makes it special.

Your supporting details must also be personalized, connected to your needs and wants. Otherwise, you're writing a book report on the school. It needs to be about you!

Vague (not specific) and impersonal (not personal) supporting details raise red flags.

Continuing with our "why statement 1" above, let's look at some supporting details that raise red flags.

Example of red-flag supporting details

Education has been my portal to a better life, which is why I have always dreamed of being a teacher—a role that will allow me to support students the way so many teachers have supported me. Junction College's secondary education program is the ideal vehicle to pursue this long-held goal. The college has incredible, esteemed professors and rich coursework that aligns with my future goals. Additionally, the education department is filled with sophisticated students who share my dreams of making a great education something that all students can attain no matter their backgrounds. Finally, I am drawn to Junction College's collaborative learning environment, in which students are able to grow together and push one another.

Analysis: Red flags! All I see are fancy buzzwords and empty fluff. These are vague comments that could apply to almost any school. Furthermore, they are impersonal: not one shows why *this* college in particular is a good fit for *this* particular applicant.

Now let's look at a paragraph whose supporting details are both specific and personal.

Example of specific, personal supporting details

Education has been my portal to a better life, which is why I have always dreamed of being a teacher—a role that will allow me to support students the way so many teachers have supported me. Junction College's secondary education program is the ideal vehicle to pursue this long-held goal. For me, it started with the facilities. During my visit last October, I connected with Associate Professor of Secondary Education Dr. Boris Tittles, who took time to show me Starling Educator Center. Its astounding physical beauty wasn't as impressive as what it stands for: a commitment to training great teachers. Junction is the first college I've encountered where the secondary education program doesn't feel, well, secondary. Talking with Dr. Tittles, I learned about the TEACH-OUT program, which would allow me to begin assisting in a local classroom as early as sophomore year and student-teaching by senior year—putting me on track to teach in a public school right after graduation. Along the way, I would hope to secure the coveted Junction Education Fellowship and perform research alongside Dr. Tittles and his peers, Dr. Damon Porter and Dr. Maggio McCaphrey. If accepted to Junction College, I would relish the chance to learn from and work with these academic giants, who make me proud to be a future educator.

Analysis: This paragraph is filled with specific supporting details about what makes Junction College special. Further, every supporting detail is personalized; the writer explains why it matters to him. He has done his research and clearly wants to attend. This is a rather long paragraph, but remember, if you have a top match point, you can spend more words on it.

Step Four: <u>Articulate</u> Your Gut Feeling

A college choice often comes down to a gut feeling, a hard-to-explain sense that a college is right for you. I'm asking you to put it into words. It will be helpful both for your introductory and conclusion paragraphs.

Structuring your essay

What follows is just a suggested structure; you don't have to follow it exactly or at all. In general I discourage you from thinking there is a formula for writing. Choose a structure that works for you.

First paragraph

- Open with a strong first sentence; "hook" the reader.
- Jump into your first, most important match point with its "why statement."

- Flesh out your why statement with 3–5 specific and personal supporting details.

*It's okay to spend more time (even an extra paragraph) discussing your top match point.

Remaining body paragraphs

- Open with a transition sentence that smoothly moves to your next match point.
- Jump into your next match point with its "why statement."
- Flesh out your "why statement" with 3–5 specific and personal supporting details.

Conclusion

- You can, but don't have to, restate what you've written in different words.
- Share your gut feeling—that "thing" driving you to this school.
- Reiterate what makes this college special.

Final advice

Don't use the same "why us?" essay for multiple schools. That's the opposite of providing specific supporting details. Also, you might forget to change the previous school's name. Then you'll be in trouble.

College Essays That Worked

Below are three personal statements that worked. One is an example of "going deep" and two are examples of "going wide." For each essay, I have included comments to point out what, specifically, made these essays great as well as a short overall analysis. You can view more essays online at: www.masteryprep.com/cpb-resources. Password is *CollegeSuccess*.

Essay #1: Deep Narrative

I definitely didn't become an adult when I was five. But it's important I talk about a certain day when I was five in order to make sense of the day I did.

Recently, a freshman at my high school was sitting at my lunch table and started talking about 9/11. By the way he was talking, that infamous day was ancient history to him – something he read about in a textbook, something he expected no one at the table to remember personally.

I closed my eyes. I was downtown that day:

It is my third day of Kindergarten at P.S. 89 and the principal has called a sudden assembly. My class lazily files into the auditorium. The principal tells us something bad has happened a few blocks away at the World Trade Center and before I can process this, my dad races into the building, completely disheveled. He grabs my older brother David and me and together we speed out of the school and now I'm scared. Looking up, I see a skyscraper I have passed every day, now with a massive, gaping hole. It's black and red and it almost seems like I'm looking at a picture except I also know my younger brother Andrew attends pre-school at the WTC. The cops wouldn't let us go south to get him, so we start walking, then racing, north. I'm not crying. I feel outside my feelings. The air is thick with something – soot? Dust? My dad tries to rip his dress shirt into squares to cover our mouths, but it won't rip. A stranger walking near us instantly rips his own. Now we are running, me on my dad's shoulders. Now we are alongside a lady we know. Now we are on a bus being handed construction masks which I do not want to wear because they make me feel like maybe I'll suffocate.

Now it's night. We still haven't heard from my mom or little brother and it is 11pm and we can't go home, if our home is even still standing in Battery Park City. We are staying with the lady we were running with. I am watching TV on a blow-up mattress when finally she calls: my mom. She and my younger brother were evacuated by the Army Corps of Engineers and were safe. She had a late start and had not dropped Andrew off after all...

Style: Strong opening. Why even suggest you became an adult when you were five? The abnormality hooks the reader.

Content: One main point. In clear, simple language, she tells us what she's about to do.

Content: Before she dives into the next scene, she gives us context so we aren't lost.

Style: The writing is lean, simple, and clear. To this point, she's used only one advanced vocabulary word, "infamous." Otherwise, she's just setting up an interesting story.

Style: Descriptive writing gives us a picture of the tired children moseying to the auditorium.

Content/Style: Zooms out from "going deep" to share a reflection, which strengthens her story. With simple language, she shares a complex feeling we all know: being disconnected from any recognizable emotion.

Content: In this paragraph, she "goes deep." We are right there with her, each sentence taking us forward a few minutes or even seconds.

Content: For two paragraphs, the writer escaped into a memory she detailed for us. Now she continues from the opening scene.

...Back at the lunch table, I opened my eyes. Someone had clearly just mentioned that I had been there that day. The freshman looked at me with wide eyes. He asked what it was like.

I could have mentioned my fear, the horror of losing possessions, the paralyzing dread wondering whether my mom and little brother were alive. Instead, I found myself talking about the man who ripped his shirt, the construction worker who forced me to wear a mask so I could stay healthy, the generosity of the woman who gave us a place to stay. As a result of that day, my life path was completely altered. I still wonder what direction it would have taken had I not been forced to leave the city.

Content: One main point!

And yet the day I became an adult wasn't that day in 2001. It wasn't when I was 5. It was in that lunchroom when I was 17, when I realized that I can choose how to remember something. I can choose to find meaning in that day, not in the horror but in other people's kindness. I can't choose what to remember but I can choose how to remember.

Content: Resolution and reflection. She shares what she learned and gives us a feeling of closure that she's growing up and everything will be alright.

It is probably too soon to truly say I am an adult. But something did change in me that day and I feel different – I look forward to continuing to change, to sharing my experiences, and to learning what other people have to teach me.

Analysis

Style: She opens strong, hooking us. Her language is simple and clear. She uses advanced vocabulary sparingly, flexing her intellect just enough and otherwise relying on detailed storytelling. With descriptive language, she allows the reader to access a powerful memory and the thoughts and feelings she had during it.

Content: Her story is easy to follow because it's held together by one main point. At the start, we think that main point is about becoming an adult. At the end, we learn it's more specific: she became an adult after realizing she's in control of how she processes memories, even the toughest ones. She spends her essay proving that point, "going deep" into two scenes. Her supporting details prove two things: this was a terrible day, but also, people helped out. This evidence proves her main point about how we choose to look into our past. Finally, the essay is personal. It invites us into a private experience, making the piece more interesting and enabling us to connect with her.

Essay #2: Wide Narrative

Her seventy-year-old fingers felt like raw fish sticks on my eight-year-old cheek.

Style: Strong opening. Descriptive language inserts us into a scene.

Nenana's sweetness belied an intensity she only revealed in moments like this. "You're different than them," she said. "They will look at you differently." "I know, Nenana," I replied, "I'm black." I expected something less obvious. I boarded the bus on the first day of second grade, aware of my skin, hair and the other traits that showed my colored half. But I ignored what Nenana saw: I would never fit in. I wonder if she knew the extent to which this would be true.

Content: Even though this is a wide narrative, he opens by "going deep," thrusting us into a specific scene.

Content: One main point! We know what the essay will be about.

I grew up in Grand Junction, Colorado, with my mom, great-grandmother and older sister, who are white, and two younger sisters, who are biracial. My dad, who is black, was mostly absent from my life until high school. I grew up around all white people, but I did not act "white." I acted like the people around me; they just happened to be white. I thought they acted equally like me. But in elementary and middle school, surface-level differences – like being overweight or wearing glasses – are enough to make students feel isolated.

Content: After the intro, he shares some background info so we know what's going on. This paragraph begins the long, wide narrative.

Content: Don't be all talk. He lays out several examples.

In Colorado, I was the black kid. I was much more than my appearance, but still, I was the black kid. My friends reminded me of it. Michael would flippantly say the n-word, while Jack spouted unoriginal fried chicken jokes. I was not overly athletic, but my basketball coaches still insisted I "do something" when we were losing. Even though they did not mean to hurt me, they isolated me. Worse, I played no part in constructing my identity. It was built by my peers – by their thoughtless comments and unwelcoming stares. It was built by default. After eighth grade, I was happy this might end. We were moving to Cleburne, Texas to help my older sister who had proved unfit to live on her own. Being new would be hard, but I looked forward to being around people who looked like me, and thus, would accept me.

Content: Don't be all talk. He gives another example of surface-level differences.

Content: This paragraph covers the first 12 years of his life. #widenarrative

Unfortunately, I was still an outsider in Texas; my differences just took on a new meaning. My school had black, white, and Mexican students, so whereas before I was ostracized for one reason, in Cleburne I was excluded for many. White students felt just like those in Colorado, while black students made sure I never forgot I was, in fact, not black. My caramel skin earned me the nickname "primo." If not for my subpar Spanish, I could have been Mexican. I was confused. The eight years before, I might as well have had a forehead tattoo reading, "I am black." Now, kids who looked like me did not accept my actions, and kids who acted like me did not accept my looks. Again, my peers' comments were bricks that both weighed me down and built my identity. They did not intend to hurt me, but they isolated me nonetheless. Moving again only made fitting in harder.

Content: Opening sentence introduces his next life chapter. #widenarrative

Content: Zooms out from storytelling to share his reflections and analysis. This develops his evidence and strengthens his main point about never fitting in.

Style: This sounds natural. He has already proven he's intelligent, so there is no risk here. He is just saying what's on his mind - and it works.

At the end of freshman year, my parents agreed: I needed to "become a man," and this could only happen living with one. I moved to Baton Rouge to live with my dad, whom I last saw in seventh grade. He did not want to teach me to be a man but a black man, and he chose a school for that purpose. Scotlandville, my current school, has 1300 students, three white and the rest black. I was not among the three, but I was "white," and skin tone was least of my concerns. I rose to among the top in my class, improved my communication, and acted respectfully. These were "white" habits that further distanced me from my black peers. My parents taught me that fitting in should not cost doing the right thing. So, I kept doing the right thing. But the right thing, frankly, sucked.

Content: His conclusion is a reflection. He shares what he has learned.

Junior year, I began listening to Childish Gambino. His songs said what I wanted to: "I'm sorry man, but I act me; I don't act "black," whatever that be." I recognize it is cheesy to cite a song lyric as my inspiration, but I'm just being honest. It made me realize I let others' views define me, and thus my isolation was partially self-inflicted. Objectively, I did not have it easy. Besides being a social misfit, I grew up on, and still depend on, food stamps. But it could be worse. At Scotlandville, my light skin lets me act "white," which apparently, and sadly, means making good grades and smart decisions. It depresses me terribly to imagine the alternative: fitting in. My darker peers are enslaved by the lowest academic and social expectations. Now that I have gotten over myself, I hope to help some of those students care less about what others think.

Content: We are left with a closure, a positive feeling of what's to come.

Analysis

Style: Again we see language that's simple, clear, and easy to understand. A sprinkling of advanced vocabulary words, used correctly, shows us he's intelligent but not doing the most. Though this is a wide narrative, his language is no less specific and descriptive. He still paints a picture with phrases like, "fingers felt like raw fish sticks" and others.

Content: His story is easy to follow because it is held together by one point: that he has always struggled to fit in because of his race and his peers' misperceptions of it. He introduces this point in the first paragraph and uses his body paragraphs to prove it. His body paragraphs are filled with evidence—concrete examples of what "not fitting in" looked like in each phase and setting of his life. He also includes his analysis; at various points he shares thoughts and feelings linking the evidence to the central argument. His comments in the conclusion about taking responsibility for his identify show maturity and self-reflection. The reader is left imagining a humble, self-aware young man who doesn't feel sorry for himself.

Essay #3: Wide Montage

I spent my entire childhood engulfed in the world of my imagination. I spent countless hours draped in taffeta gowns of bubblegum pink, ocean blue and sunshiny yellow as a medieval princess: Lady Michelle. My castle was a nearby church and my moat was the concrete road. The jester? My brother Tom. I slipped a patch over my eye and sailed onto my bed, now Blackbeard's pirate ship, my treasure map drawn onto my wall in magic marker until Admiral Tom came in and revealed it to the king and queen. Other days my lush backyard became dotted with tumbleweeds as I put on a hat to become a cowboy in the Wild West chasing the Indian Sitting Tom.

My saloon sheltered in my tree house. As I've grown into adolescence, my days of endless time travel have almost ended, my plaid skirt replacing the whimsical dresses and to-do lists replacing the hours of play. But not quite, my imagination and my world have one final fortress: Strawbery Banke.

At Strawbery Banke, a history museum comprised of restored houses, I exchange my skinny jeans for an empire waist dress complete with a bonnet and my world of imagination reopens. I am Mary Chase and my world is 1814, a time of James Madison and the war of 1812. Maybe, if you're lucky, I'll let you, the museum visitor, in on my secret: I flirt with the boys through the language of my fan. If I'm waving my fan quickly, I'm interested, but if I fan myself slowly? Run! My world morphs, and my empire waist dress turns into saddle shoes and a blouse and skirt cut from the same cloth. Before you know it, 1945 is in full swing and now I am Helen Jalicki, my life filled with radios, WWII and lines drawn up the backs of my legs with eyeliner pencils since nylons are rationed. But don't tell my mother! I look at the sailors over the fence of the navy shipyard too...my mother probably shouldn't find out about that either! I trade in my saddle shoes for an A-line skirt with crinoline itching my thighs, now Betty Quackenbush's. Enter my world of 1955 and watch my nifty TV as the Cold War shivers on outside. I'll show you my Elvis record, slightly warped since I sleep with it under my pillow so my mom won't find it.

Style: Strong opening. In this montage essay, her lens is her imagination. This sentence helps us make sense of what would otherwise seem like a random list of elements.

Style: Descriptive language is key for a montage essay. Her adjectives create vivid images for the reader.

Friendly note: It is discriminatory and insensitive to refer to Native Americans as "Indians."

Content: Theme is one of the "big three" for a montage essay. Here she introduces it: a love of history.

Style: Speaking to the reader creates a feeling of familiarity, making the essay more personal and interesting.

Content: Geek out! She is clearly a history geek, which is awesome! If you have a similarly deep passion, show it off!

Content: Even as she jumps from element to element, she stops to analyze the evidence. Here her reflection tells us she feels empowered by recreating history through her imagination.

The worlds of my imagination are released, at Strawbery Banke, from the confines of Hardy-Weinberg equations and conjugating the subjunctive case. Here I can recreate those worlds, but instead of just inviting my older brother in, I invite hundreds of strangers, not just into the museum, but into my world, my imagination, my spin on history. There are 300 years of American history and old guys with PhDs have already written the history books. But now I get to write history from the viewpoints of 17-year-old girls. I get my chance to say yes, Eisenhower matters but so does Betty. Mary, Helen and Betty matter just as much as Hamilton, FDR and MacArthur. When I open up my little world of history to the visitors, I realize the power of the individual. Individuals matter because all of them can open up their worlds to others and share history. Every individual who has ever lived has influenced history and left a mark. They've mattered. They mattered when they were alive; they still matter today. Maybe I'll end up a homemaker like Helen with four kids and a doting husband or maybe I'll follow my dreams and end up in Zambia living and breathing my passion: public health. But either way my little world and my story are so much bigger than I am because they are something shared, something communal. My world and my story are pieces of the pointillist painting of the human condition: history.

Content: Though this is a montage, it ends with closure. She shares her reflections on what history means to her. She lets us in on her uneasiness about growing up but still gives a feeling of resolution about her future.

Analysis

Style: Montage essays depend on descriptive writing. Her elements—pieces of history in her imagination—are deeply personal, yet she lets us into her world by painting vivid pictures. At the same time, her language is simple and clear. In classic montage style, her essay jumps around from one element to the next, but the elements don't feel disconnected. She sews them together with phrases like, "…my world of imagination reopens" and "the worlds of my imagination are released."

Content: Her theme is history, with maybe a touch of growing up. Her lens is her imagination. It's how we make sense of her elements, the many stops on her journey back in time. This lens is key, since she isn't doing a book report; no, each experience is personalized. She spends most of her words on elements but stops now and then to connect them with reflection and analysis. This keeps the essay smooth, even while she rattles off elements. Her conclusion grounds us in the broader theme of history. Her final sentences keep us in touch with her lens of imagination, and they offer a resolution: she has her own place in the past and is excited about her future.

How to Write a Great Activity Description

Extracurricular involvement is one of the Big Five things colleges want to see. It matters a lot, which means it also matters *how* you describe the activities you participated in.

Most application platforms allow applicants to list up to ten activities and include the following information:

1. Activity name
2. Activity type (e.g., sports, arts, community service, faith-based, etc.)
3. Roles held (e.g., president, captain, treasurer, secretary, etc.)
4. Length of commitment (grades you participated, hours per week, weeks per year)
5. Short description of activity and your role in it

The activity description is not just a chance to highlight your extracurricular involvement. Your short descriptions (#5) are further opportunities to flex your writing skills and cleverness. Indeed it takes cleverness to describe your participation in just 150 characters (including spaces), the limit the Common App allows for each activity. Other college and scholarship application platforms have similarly short character limits.

Below are nine tips—five on content, four on style—for crafting an excellent activity description.

Content Tips

1. **Include most impressive info:** Use your limited characters to describe, very specifically, your responsibilities, contributions, promotions, and achievements. If you had to apply or try out for the activity, point that out.

Activity Type	Participation grade levels	Position/leadership description and organization name, if applicable:
Swimming	9,10,11,12	McKinley Varsity Team - Captain
Please describe this activity, including what you accomplished and any recognition you received, etc.		
Bad (focuses on unimpressive info): Race in swim meets once per week for 12-week season; during practice, swim, lift weights, and build flexibility		
Good (focuses on most impressive info): Captain: lead captain's practices, coordinate meet logistics, work with coach on training plan; awards: Most Dedicated (11, 12); event: 50m freestyle		

2. **Avoid redundancy:** Don't repeat in the short description anything you've covered in another field. The exception is if you held a special role and are describing what, specifically, it entailed.

Activity Type	Participation grade levels	Position/leadership description and organization name, if applicable:
Music, Instru-mental	9,10,11,12	Marching Band, Section Leader - Lower Brass
Please describe this activity, including what you accomplished and any recognition you received, etc.		
Bad (repeats info from other fields): Serve as lower brass section leader of school marching band for all of high school career; as veteran, support other section leaders; fix instruments		
Good/acceptable redundancy (adds new, key info, explains leadership role): Section leader: ensure participants represent section proudly through play, dress, posture, energy; as veteran, support other leaders; fix instruments		

3. **If they don't know, tell them:** If the activity isn't self-explanatory, provide a very brief explanation so the reader knows what you're talking about.

Activity Type	Participation grade levels	Position/leadership description and organization name, if applicable:
Other (Community Org)	9,10,11,12	Baton Rouge Youth Coalition (BRYC), Ambassador *(Not enough characters to say anything else.)*
Please describe this activity, including what you accomplished and any recognition you received, etc.		
Bad (falsely assumes reader knows what BRYC is): Selected as Ambassador to recruit new Fellows and lead tours		
Good (explains what BRYC is): Selected from competitive applicant pool as "Fellow" in after-school college prep program; chosen as Ambassador to recruit new Fellows and lead tours		

4. **Start with top activities:** List your activities in descending order of importance, starting with the ones that matter most to you.

5. **When in doubt, list it:** Even though you will have 2-3 activities that stand out among the rest, I suggest using all available spots. Every non-academic commitment counts, including family responsibilities and work. If you follow my tips, no activity description will read as insignificant.

Style Tips

1. **Be concise:** If you're clever, you can say a ton in 150 characters. Start with a separate document. List everything you want to include. Then figure out how to fit it in. As long as you're consistent (next tip), you can utilize fragments and other creative measures to cut characters. Having an expert editor would help!

Activity Type	Participation grade levels	Position/leadership description and organization name, if applicable:
Work (Paid)	11,12	McDonald's, Fry Cook & Crew Trainer

Please describe this activity, including what you accomplished and any recognition you received, etc.
Bad (too wordy; does not utilize fragments or punctuation to shorten): I did well as fry cook and was eventually promoted to Crew Trainer; here I was charged with teaching others about not only cooking but customer service
Good (utilizes fragments, abbreviations, and punctuation to say more): Standout fry cook; after 1 yr. promoted to Crew Trainer: taught employees cooking, customer service; awards: Employee of Month (4x), Golden Arch (2x)

2. **Be consistent:** Use abbreviations and punctuation to cut characters; just be consistent in how you do so across all descriptions. Same goes for capitalization. I have been consistent in all "good" examples so far. Check out how the "bad" example below <u>violates</u> how I have been punctuating and capitalizing all along.

Activity Type	Participation grade levels	Position/leadership description and organization name, if applicable:
Athletics: JV/ Varsity	10,11,12	Varsity Basketball - Captain & Point Guard **Bad:** In the other activities, a comma separated the activity name and my role. In this case, I used a dash, which is not consistent.

Please describe this activity, including what you accomplished and any recognition you received, etc.
Bad (punctuation, capitalization inconsistent with other sections): Captain - led captain's practices; designed weightlifting program; set example for team; awards: most improved (10), MVP (12), sportsmanship award.
Good (punctuation, capitalization consistent with other sections): Captain: led captain's practices, designed weightlifting program, set example for team; awards: Most Improved (10), MVP (12), Sportsmanship Award

How was the "bad" example inconsistent? In all other "good" examples, I...

- Used a colon, not a dash, after a position name to describe its duties
- Used commas, not semicolons, to separate position duties in a list
- Capitalized all award names
- Did not end the description with a period

3. **Use strong, specific verbs:** Just as you would on a résumé, use strong verbs that express exactly what you've done. The right verbs can make what you've done sound even more impressive than it is, which is fine!

If you volunteered at an after-school program helping kids, say "tutored" or "mentored" rather than "helped." If you oversee others at work, say "manage" or "supervise" rather than "worked with."

4. **Flex your vocabulary:** The activity description is another chance to show off your vocabulary. In the process, you'll sound even more impressive than you are, which is great! Don't overdo it, though. Advanced vocabulary words are like salt; a few pinches will do.

Good: As captain, told teammates when to be at bus and what to wear for games.

Better: As captain, communicated game logistics to teammates.

Example Activity Description

Music: Instrumental

9, 10, 11, 12	**Marching Band - Section Leader, Lower Brass**
School, Break, Year	Section leader: ensure participants represent section proudly through play, dress, posture, energy; as veteran, support other leaders; fix instruments
25 hr/wk, 36 wk/yr	

Other Club/Activity

9, 10, 11, 12	**Baton Rouge Youth Coalition (BRYC) Ambassador**
School, Year	Selected from large, competitive applicant pool as a "Fellow" in after-school college access program; selected as Ambassador to recruit new Fellows
5 hr/wk, 40 wk/yr	

Music: Vocal

10, 11, 12	**Talented Music, Vocalist**
School	Learned various musical styles and performed countless recitals at my high school, local elementary and middle schools, and greater community events
3 hr/wk, 28 wk/yr	

Music: Instrumental

10, 11, 12	**A Cappella Choir, Vocalist**
School	Performed numerous concerts at my high school and in the greater Baton Rouge community
3.5 hr/wk, 36 wk/yr	

Other Club/Activity

10, 11, 12	**McKinley High Poetry Club, Member**
School	Attend workshops on different writing and performance styles; this year will participate with school slam team for annual citywide contest
2 hr/wk, 28 wk/yr	

Other Club/Activity

10, 11	**BRYC Slam Poetry Team, Member**
School	Wrote original pieces, practiced w/ team to prep for citywide contest; team excelled, didn't advance due to violation: too many poets in group piece
4 hr/wk, 28 wk/yr	

Community Service (Volunteer)

9,10, 11, 12	**LSU Fanatics, Volunteer**
School	Raised ~$100,000 over four years by selling Louisiana State University merchandise during home football games; recognized for stellar customer service
10 hr/wk, 7 wk/yr	

Community Service (Volunteer)

11	**Helping Youth Prepare for Excellence (HYPE), Buddy**
School	Mentored and tutored elementary school students through HYPE, an after-school enrichment program administered by a local church
4 hr/wk, 15 wk/yr	

Internship

12	**Baton Rouge Youth Coalition (BRYC) Apprentice**
School	Aid to Managing Director of Academics: assist with test and homework grading, data entry, space upkeep, and completion of administrative tasks
4 hr/wk, 30 wk/yr	

Work (Paid)

11	**McDonald's - Fry Cook, Crew Trainer**
School, Break, Year	Cooked golden french fries while delivering top-notch customer service; as Crew Trainer, provided introductory and ongoing training to new employees
20 hr/wk, 40 wk/yr	

How to Handle an Interview

Some colleges offer interviews as part of the application process. Some, but few, require them; other schools don't offer them at all.

If you can, I recommend you interview. Why?

- **It probably won't hurt:** Unless you do something particularly unimpressive, an interview won't hurt you. If you do well, though, a positive report from the interviewer could boost your chances.

- **If you're on the cusp:** If your GPA and ACT/SAT score are below the school's averages for incoming freshman, a strong interview could make the case that you deserve to be admitted.

- **Demonstrated interest:** Remember, some colleges really want you to want them back. (Don't we all?) Scheduling an interview, especially when it's optional, shows you care.

- **Tell your whole story:** An interview is a good chance to further explain any special circumstances—like a temporary dip in your grades—that it may have been difficult to address in your written application.

- **It's good practice:** You will have many interviews in your future. Being a good interviewer is a huge asset in this cold, lonely world.

Setting up your interview

When arranging your interview, show off your professional email skills and make life easy for the interviewer. Speaking as an interviewer, my evaluation of students begins before we meet. I am impressed when students communicate considerately and respect my time. Here's an example of how you could respond when an interviewer reaches out.

Sample response after an interviewer emails you to arrange an interview:

Dear (interviewer name),

It's great to hear from you! I appreciate you reaching out. Below are several days/times that would work for me to meet. If none of these works for you, just let me know and I will send more options.

- Tuesday, January 27 @ 5pm
- Wednesday January 28 @ 4pm
- Thursday, January 29 @ 3pm
- Friday, January 30 @ 5pm

How do you feel about meeting at the Starbucks on Third Street?

I look forward to getting to know one another, explaining why I want to attend (college name), and learning about your experience there.

Sincerely,

(your name)

Dos and Don'ts of Interviewing

Do		
Before	**During**	**After**
• Rehearse with a mentor, parent, teacher, or friend. • Research the college. Be prepared to share, in detail, why you want to attend. • Email your interviewer to confirm the appointment the day before. • Turn off and put away your cell phone. • Be five minutes early. • Dress professionally. • Bring a few hard copies of your résumé, notebook, and a pen.	• Open with a firm handshake while smiling and looking the interviewer in the eyes. • Maintain eye contact. Don't stare, though; there's a difference. • Smile frequently. Don't look creepy, though; there's a difference. • Ask questions! Especially ones you can't easily find answers to. • Take notes! Write things you want to remember and questions to ask later. • End with a firm handshake, thank you, and smile.	• Send a professional thank-you email within 24 hours of the interview ending. • Pat yourself on the back for a job well done!

Don't
• Match your outfit to the school's colors. • Show up late. • Chew gum, eat food, slouch, or yawn. • Be negative to the point of complaining or positive to the point of <u>pandering</u>. • Respond in one-word answers. • Compliment your interviewer to score points. • Skip chances to share interesting, memorable things about yourself. • Replay the interview in your head when it's done. You did fine.

Questions you should be prepared to answer

Be prepared with thoughtful answers to the following:

1. Why do you want to attend this college?

2. What do you intend to major in, and why?

3. What are your short- and long-term goals?

4. What do you like to read, and why?

5. Whom do you admire, and why?

6. How would your friends and family describe you?

7. What are your favorite and least favorite subjects in school, and why?

8. What's your favorite activity outside of school, and why?

9. What do you do to have fun?

10. How do you spend a typical weekend?

11. What accomplishments are you most proud of, and why?

12. What local, national, or international issues concern you?

13. Is there a concept that really interests you?

14. What should I know about you I couldn't learn from your résumé or application?

15. What are your core values?

Questions you can ask

When the interviewer <u>inevitably</u> asks you if you have any questions, it looks bad if all you can do is shrug. Here are some suggestions. You should come to the table with your own questions, too.

1. How would you describe the overall culture of the school?

2. What do you think students like best about the school?

3. What do you think is something students wish they could change about the school?

4. What is the most common struggle of freshmen at the school?

5. Would you say professors make themselves available to support their students?

6. What would you have changed about your experience at the school?

7. What do most students do over the summers?

8. How do you think the school has changed in the last decade?

9. Looking back, do you feel the school prepared you for the working world?

10. How does the school show that diversity is an important part of its education?

In Summary...

- There are six types of college admissions plans: Early Decision, Early Decision 2, Restrictive Early Action, Early Action, Regular Decision, and Rolling Admission.

- If you apply Early Decision or Early Decision 2 and the school accepts you, you're obligated to attend. The other admissions plans are not binding, but some are more restrictive than others.

- Your personal statement is a way for you to tell your whole story and show why a school would want you added to their student population. Spend time brainstorming topics and stories that describe your personality, your interests, your future aspirations, etc.

- Ask your mentor to read over your personal statement and give you honest feedback.

- You can see more examples of winning school essays online: www.masteryprep.com/cpb-resources. The password is *CollegeSuccess*.

Special College Processes

If You Are an Undocumented Immigrant

Undocumented immigrants—students born outside the U.S. who are not American citizens or legal residents—face significant barriers to college. What follows is a basic overview, focusing on the three main dimensions of the college application process that will be unique for undocumented students:

1. Admission
2. Tuition
3. Financial Aid

Admission

There is no federal or state law prohibiting undocumented immigrants from attending U.S. colleges. However, different colleges have different institutional policies on admitting undocumented students.

For instance, certain four-year state colleges in Virginia require applicants to submit proof of citizenship or legal residency and refuse admission to students without documentation. On the other hand, there are some colleges that not only readily admit undocumented students but support them with robust financial aid. We will discuss those below.

Tuition

Many state institutions charge undocumented students out-of-state (i.e., higher) tuition fees, even if the student is a long-time resident of the state. As of 2015, the following states allow undocumented students to pay in-state tuition if they attend the state's public institutions.

1. California
2. Colorado
3. Connecticut
4. Florida
5. Illinois
6. Kansas
7. Maryland
8. Minnesota
9. Nebraska
10. New Jersey
11. New Mexico
12. New York
13. Oregon
14. Texas
15. Utah
16. Washington

As mentioned above, there are a handful of very selective colleges that admit undocumented students *and* meet 100% of their financial need through some combination of grants, student employment, scholarships, and loans. They are:

1. Amherst College
2. Bates College
3. Bowdoin College
4. Bryn Mawr College
5. Brown University
6. Colby College
7. Columbia University
8. Cornell University
9. Dartmouth College
10. Duke University
11. Emory University
12. Harvard College
13. Haverford College
14. Macalester College
15. Massachusetts Institute of Technology
16. Middlebury College
17. Oberlin College
18. Occidental College
19. Pomona College
20. Princeton University
21. Rice University
22. Smith College
23. Swarthmore College
24. Tufts University
25. University of Chicago
26. University of Notre Dame
27. University of Pennsylvania
28. Vassar College
29. Wellesley College
30. Wesleyan University
31. Williams College
32. Yale University

Financial Aid

Let's start with the bad news.

- Undocumented students—including those with Deferred Action for Childhood Arrivals (DACA) status—are not eligible to receive federally funded student financial aid, including loans, grants, scholarships, and work-study employment.

- Most states do not offer state financial aid to undocumented students.

- Most private scholarship organizations require applicants to be U.S. citizens or legal residents.

Now for the good news:

- As mentioned above, there are states that grant state financial aid to students who qualify for in-state tuition.

- As mentioned above, there are colleges that offer generous financial aid packages to the undocumented students they admit.

- Some private scholarship organizations do not require applicants to be U.S. citizens or legal residents. In other words, there are scholarships available to undocumented students. Below is a resource for you to check out—but don't let this be the end of your search!

http://blog.collegegreenlight.com/blog/scholarships-for-undocumented-students/

If You Are Homeschooled

The college application process for homeschool students is largely the same as that for non-homeschool students. Still, there are a few things homeschool students should pay special attention to.

- **Make sure you're taking the right courses:** In "High School Courses Colleges Want to See," you'll find a breakdown of classes almost all colleges will expect you to have taken. Make sure you're meeting these requirements, but don't stop there. Colleges also want to see that you've challenged yourself. Homeschool students can take advanced classes at a local college or online. To learn more about online options, visit www.hslda. com.

- **Pay attention to special requirements:** Colleges may have special requirements for homeschool students. Make sure you're aware of and fulfilling these. It doesn't hurt to call the admissions office to double check.

- **Find colleges that are homeschool-friendly:** Some colleges—like Georgia Tech (Atlanta, GA), Beloit College (Beloit, WI), and Northeastern University (Boston, MA)—are known for being particularly homeschool-friendly. A Google search will lead you to other such schools.

- **Test scores and essays are key:** Your GPA is still critical, but it's difficult for a college to know exactly how rigorous any homeschool education is. This puts other application components in the spotlight. Strong standardized test scores (SAT/ACT, SAT II Subject Tests, AP Exams) and essays demonstrate not only that you're #1 in your class but that you stack up well nationally.

- **Get active outside of school:** It's important that homeschool students get involved outside the classroom. First, colleges expect it. Second, participation in organized activities gives homeschool students a chance to meet friends, learn teamwork, and develop leadership skills. Finally, homeschool students need strong recommendation letters, which they can request from activity leaders.

- **Secure strong recommendation letters:** Recommendation letters are particularly important for homeschool students. Some colleges may accept parent recommendation letters, but it's best to submit letters from other adults who know you well, like coaches, mentors, and job supervisors.

- **Take advantage of your interview:** Interviews are usually mandatory for homeschool students. Even if a college only recommends it, go for it! An interview is another chance for homeschool students to squash any doubt they belong at that college.

Resources for homeschool students

There is a growing body of resources online for homeschool students and their parents.

- **Home School Legal Defense Association (HSLDA)** – This organization advocates for homeschool students and has great college admissions resources. (www.hslda.org)

- **MIT Admissions Advice for Homeschooled Applicants** – Incredible advice for homeschool students about preparing for college and navigating the admissions process. (http://mitadmissions.org/blogs/entry/homeschooled_applicants)

- **"And What About College?"** – A great book by Cafi Cohen about how homeschooling leads to admission to some of the best colleges.

- **College Admissions Office** – No one can give you more reliable answers about an admissions process than the people in charge of it. Don't hesitate to call.

If You Have a Disability

Students with disabilities have a slightly different college application process than their nondisabled peers.

Are you a student with a disability?

According to the Americans with Disability Act, a student is considered to have a disability if they meets at least one of the following three conditions:

- Has a documented physical or mental impairment that substantially limits one or more major life activities

- Has a record of this impairment

- Is perceived as having such an impairment

Physical disabilities include impairments of speech, vision, hearing and/or mobility as well as diabetes, asthma, multiple sclerosis, heart disease, cancer, mental illness, and cerebral palsy.

Learning disabilities are commonly recognized as impairments in one or more of the following areas: oral and/or written expression, listening comprehension, basic reading skills, reading comprehension, mathematical calculation or problem-solving. Learning disabilities may also include challenges with sustained attention, time management, and/or social interaction.

Should you receive testing accommodations?

If you have a learning disability or other impairment that will make it difficult for you to perform well on the SAT or ACT under traditional testing conditions, you should request testing accommodations. Accommodations will vary based on a student's needs, but here are some common ones:

- Extended time

- Use of a computer

- Sign language interpreters

- Extra or extended breaks

- Special presentation (e.g., larger print, colored paper, Braille)

- Test read aloud

- Special time and day for test

- Special setting for test

Where should you go to college?

The Americans with Disabilities Act requires colleges to ensure all students can fully participate in the programs they offer. But some colleges take this <u>charge</u> more seriously than others. Students with disabilities and their parents need to make sure the colleges they apply to will meet their needs. Here are some colleges known for their support of students with disabilities:

- Augsburg College
- Baylor University
- Curry College
- DePaul University
- Flagler College
- Franklin Pierce College
- Landmark College
- Lesley University
- Loras College
- Lynn University
- Mercyhurst College
- Mitchell College
- Schreiner University
- Southern Illinois University (Carbondale)

- Southern Methodist University
- Texas Tech University
- University of Arizona
- University of California Berkeley
- University of Denver
- University of Houston
- University of Indianapolis
- University of Montana
- University of the Ozarks
- University of Tulsa
- Westfield State University
- Westminster College (Missouri)
- Whittier College

Will disclosing your disability hurt your admissions chances?

Colleges can't ask if you have a disability, so it's up to you to volunteer that information. Here are several reasons why you should <u>disclose</u> your disability:

- It's part of who you are and nothing to be ashamed of.
- If a school doesn't admit you because of it, you shouldn't go there.
- A disability is a form of diversity that can help you stand out.
- It's only fair for colleges to understand how your disability has impacted you.
- If you get in, the college can connect you to helpful resources.

What about scholarships?

There are numerous scholarships specifically for students with disabilities. Below are a few examples. Keep in mind that colleges may offer institutional scholarships specifically for students with disabilities.

- Marion Huber Learning Through Listening Award - $6,000
- The Jake Jones Memorial Scholarship for the Learning Disabled - $500
- Krawitz Scholarship - $500
- Hy and Greta Berkowitz Scholarship for Students with Disabilities - $500
- Linda Cowden Memorial Scholarship - $1,000
- National Federation of the Blind Scholarship - $7,000
- AmeriGlide Achiever Scholarship - $500

These are just a handful. Get on the internet and find more!

If You Want To Attend a Military College

What is a Military/Service Academy?

The United States service academies, also known as the United States military academies, are federal colleges with the purpose of educating and training commissioned officers for the United States Armed Forces.

There are five service academies:

1. U.S. Military Academy, aka West Point, aka Army – West Point, New York
2. U.S. Naval Academy, aka Navy, aka Annapolis – Annapolis, Maryland
3. U.S. Coast Guard Academy – New London, Connecticut
4. U.S. Merchant Marine Academy – Kings Point, New York
5. U.S. Air Force Academy – Colorado Springs, Colorado

Why attend a service academy?

The U.S. service academies—especially West Point and Navy—are top-notch academic institutions, which makes sense: their graduates will be the men and women who protect our nation. A diploma from a service academy carries serious weight. It says you are highly intelligent and mentally and physically tough.

In addition to earning Bachelor of Science degrees, graduates of service academies have guaranteed employment in their chosen military branch. And, in exchange for a post-college service commitment of at least five years, service academy students receive free tuition, room and board, books, and medical and dental insurance. Finally, by attending a service academy, you are joining a brotherhood and sisterhood steeped in patriotism, tradition, and honor.

What is required of you after graduation from a service academy?

Depending on the academy, graduates are usually obligated to serve five years of active duty in their chosen branch plus another three years in the Reserves. In some cases, such as that of a naval pilot, the tour of duty may be longer.

How do you get into a service academy?

The application process for U.S. service academies is different from that of any other college. Meeting each academy's unique academic standards (GPA, SAT/ACT, etc.) is just one in a series of steps that a candidate must go through to be considered for acceptance.

Step 1: Meet the basic eligibility criteria:

- U.S. citizen
- Not pregnant
- Unmarried with no dependents
- At least 17 but less than 23 years old by July 1 of the year you would enter

Step 2: Pass a medical examination and physical fitness test

Step 3: Secure letters of nomination

An applicant to a service academy (except to the U.S. Coast Guard) must secure a letter of nomination from a U.S. congressperson. This is a process in and of itself. An applicant must first contact and arrange an interview with the congressperson. Depending on how it goes, the congressperson may or may not write a letter of nomination for the applicant.

Step 4: Submit your service academy application on time

The application process to U.S. service academies is intense. I have provided a basic overview but, if you're serious about this, you need to visit the website of the academy you're interested in to gain a complete understanding of its admission steps and requirements. This process is also highly selective. West Point accepts 10% of its applicants and Navy accepts 9%. Don't spend time applying unless you have good reason to believe you will be competitive.

If You Want To Be a College Athlete

Here are 10 tips to get on track towards college athletics.

1. **Get a second opinion:** Find out if you really have what it takes to compete at the next level. Ask your coach or someone who plays your sport in college.

2. **Get in compliance with NCAA requirements:** Go to www.NCAA.org to ensure you meet the eligibility criteria to compete in varsity college sports.

3. **Register online with the NCAA Eligibility Center:** Serious athletes should register with the NCAA Eligibility Center at the start of junior year. You can't play college sports or receive an athletic scholarship without registering.

4. **Attend a sports camp:** Summer sports camps are a great way to sharpen your game. College coaches sometimes attend these camps to check out the talent.

5. **Keep a resume:** Maintain a sports resume (see "How to Craft a Great Resume") with updated statistics and accomplishments. You will send this to college coaches.

6. **Get in touch with coaches:** Once you've identified which schools you're interested in, mail or email the coach a letter of interest along with your sports resume. See the sample letter below. Some colleges ask you instead to fill out a recruitment questionnaire on the team's website.

7. **Create a highlight and/or skills video:** The video can be a combination of in-game highlights and drills. Talk to a coach or current college athlete in your sport about what to include.

8. **Get on a sports recruitment website:** There are numerous websites high school athletes can use to showcase their abilities and connect with college coaches. One example is Hudl, but there are many!

9. **Understand strings attached to college scholarships:** What if you get hurt? Athletic scholarships are among the easiest to lose. As with any award, make sure you know what you must do to keep your funding.

10. **Don't let sports cloud your judgment:** You will go pro, but probably not as an athlete. Don't choose a sports program at the expense of your education. You don't want to graduate from college as a champion with no job prospects.

Example Letter of Interest to College Coaches

The example below is a template. Personalize it by sharing your history with the sport and why you believe you deserve consideration for an athletic scholarship. You may also want to share a few sentences about your interest in the college as a whole. It's okay to show a bit of personality. Coaches are looking for student-athletes who are solid people.

Your name
Street address
City, state, zip

Today's date
Full name of coach
Name of college
Address
City, state, zip

Dear Coach (*last name of coach*),

I hope this finds you well! My name is (*your name*), and I am currently a (*sophomore/junior*) at (*high school*). I'm writing to express my interest in attending (*name of college*) and being a member of your esteemed program.

Below are my current academic stats. You will find my athletic stats in the attached resume.

- GPA:
- Class Rank:
- SAT/ACT:

I am also attaching a recommendation letter from my coach and my upcoming game schedule. Finally, here is a link to my highlight video: www.hudl.com.

If you would like to contact my coach, (*high school coach's name*), (*she/he*) can be reached by email at (*email*) and by phone (*phone number*).

I would appreciate if, at your convenience, you could send me any information about the team that you think I should have. I would also love to know if you think there is a possibility of me earning an athletic scholarship. In general, I would love to know any suggestions you may have that could increase my chances of playing on your team.

Thank you so much for taking the time to read this letter. I very much hope to hear from you.

Sincerely,
(*your name*)

What You Need To Know About ROTC

This is for students interested in becoming officers in the military. It is just an overview. If you are serious about participating in ROTC, visit the website of the military branch you're considering so you can learn about its program in greater depth.

What is ROTC?

ROTC stands for Reserve Officers' Training Corps. It's a training program offered at certain colleges to prepare young men and women to be officers in the military. The Army, Air Force, and Navy have their own ROTC programs. Students interested in the Marine Corps can participate in Naval ROTC, but the Coast Guard and Merchant Marines don't currently have ROTC programs. As an ROTC cadet, you will take some military courses each year for credit, and after college you will be obligated to complete a period of service in the military.

Where is ROTC offered?

You can find out which colleges have ROTC programs by visiting the recruitment websites of the Army, Navy, and Air Force, and/or by talking to your school counselor.

What's expected of you during ROTC?

You will be required to take several military courses for credit and attend physical training sessions. Most programs will also require you to complete at least one summer program. Before you decide to become an ROTC cadet, visit the website of the branch you're considering so you can learn exactly what will be required of you.

Do cadets get to experience normal college life?

ROTC is a lifestyle. Cadets have commitments—like waking up early for training—that non-ROTC students don't have. But they still get to enjoy college life! Cadets have the same academic opportunities as their non-ROTC peers and can participate in clubs, sports, Greek organizations, and other extracurricular activities.

What's required of cadets after college?

Only cadets who receive ROTC scholarships are obligated to serve in the military after college, but most non-scholarship cadets also choose to serve. The length of a cadet's required post-college service varies by military branch, ROTC program, and scholarship status.

Most cadets take on four-year terms, but some paths require longer commitments. Before you apply for a scholarship and/or enroll in an ROTC program, make sure you fully understand what will be expected of you after graduation.

Can ROTC help you pay for college?

Yes! In fact, the military is the largest source of financial aid that is not need-based. ROTC cadets are eligible for scholarships that cover tuition, fees, and textbooks for four years, plus a monthly allowance for personal expenses. The amount of yearly funding and the number of years it will last varies by scholarship and military branch. If the ROTC scholarship doesn't cover your entire need, you can apply for regular financial aid and outside scholarships.

How can you qualify for an ROTC scholarship?

ROTC scholarships are merit-based, not need-based. Scholarship requirements will vary by military branch, but the basic requirements are as follows:

- Be a U.S. citizen
- Be between the ages of 17 and 26
- Have a high school GPA of at least 2.5
- Have a high school diploma
- Meet the physical fitness standards
- Agree to serve on active duty or in the Reserves after college
- Earn a qualifying SAT or ACT score

How can you improve your chances of earning an ROTC scholarship?

Besides earning a strong GPA and SAT/ACT score,

- **Demonstrate interest** – Reach out to local military recruitment officers as early as possible, preferably during your junior year of high school.
- **Choose the right major** – Students have a better shot at winning scholarships if they pursue majors relevant to the military, such as engineering, computer science, certain foreign languages, and nursing. Find out which majors meet the needs of your desired military branch.

When and where do you apply for ROTC scholarships?

Application deadlines vary by branch, usually falling between December 1 and January 31. Apply online at military branch websites:

- Army (goarmy.com/rotc.html)
- Navy/Marine Corps (nrotc.navy.mil)
- Air Force (www.afrotc.com)

Can you get a master's or professional degree before going on active duty?

Yes. During your fourth year, you can request an "educational delay" so you can continue your studies before going on active duty.

What if you want to quit?

You can quit ROTC at any time. If you quit before sophomore year begins, you don't have to pay back any scholarship money you received. After that, you will have to pay the money back.

In Summary...

- If you are an undocumented immigrant, you can still attend college in the U.S. You're not eligible for federally funded loans, grants, or work-study, but several states will charge you in-state tuition (which is cheaper than out-of-state tuition). Some selective colleges will even meet 100% of your financial need.

- If you are homeschooled, you need to focus extra hard on making sure you're taking the right courses to meet college admissions requirements and prepping for the ACT/SAT. Extracurricular involvement and recommedation letters can also help boost your application.

- If you have a disability, you can request testing accommodations for standardized tests; this way you can perform at your best. All colleges are required to accommodate your needs, but there are several colleges that are well known for the support they offer to students with disabilities.

- If you want to attend a military college, be sure that you can compete to get into these highly selective schools. You'll need to pass a fitness test and secure a letter of nomination from a U.S. congressperson.

- If you want to be a college athlete, there are several steps you can take now to promote your chances. Develop a highlight video of your skills, ask your coaches for recommendation letters, and send a letter of interest to the sports coach at the college you want to attend.

- If you want to join the ROTC, be prepared for a full load of military classes and physical training in addition to your college courses. You will still have an opportunity to participate in normal colllege activities, but being part of the ROTC is definitely a lifestyle.

Paying for College

How Much Will College Cost You?

Of course, the cost of attending college depends on the school you want to attend. But cost also varies by student.

The only way to know how much a college will cost you and your family is to go through the financial aid process. In this section, I'll break down how your unique cost to attend a college is determined. It's important that you understand this, because while college is expensive, it doesn't cost what you think.

There are three simple steps to figure out how much college costs.

Step 1: Determine Your Financial Need

$$
\begin{array}{r}
\text{Cost of Attendance} \\
-\quad \underline{\text{Expected Family Contribution}} \\
\text{Financial Need}
\end{array}
$$

Let's define the terms in the equation above:

- **Cost of Attendance (COA):** Also known as "sticker price," this is the number that scares most students away from applying, but it's misleading. It's just the starting cost and does not factor in the financial assistance you may receive. COA includes "hard" costs (like tuition, fees, room and board) and "soft" costs (like books and supplies). The sticker price is rarely what you end up paying; in fact, schools with higher sticker prices are often more generous.

- **Expected Family Contribution (EFC):** EFC is the minimum amount the federal government says your family should contribute toward your college education. What gives them the right?! We don't have a choice in the matter. Any student seeking financial assistance must complete the Free Application for Federal Student Aid (FAFSA), something we will discuss later. The feds put the information from your FAFSA into a formula that spits out your family's EFC. It then sends a report to each college you applied to so that they can determine your unique "financial need" using the simple formula above.

- **Financial need:** When a college subtracts your EFC from its cost of attendance, it produces your unique financial need. This figure isn't what you'll pay; rather it helps the college determine your financial aid package, a combination of grants, loans, and work-study available to you. This package may or may not cover your actual financial need; you are responsible for covering any leftover costs.

Step 2: Determine Unmet Need

Your unmet need is the amount of financial need left over after a college has awarded your financial aid.

Financial Need

−   Financial Aid (grants, loans, work-study)

Unmet Need

Step 3: Determine Net Price

Your "net price" is the amount you will have to pay in a given school year.

Unmet Need

+   EFC

Net Price

Example

Let's say that after completing your FAFSA, the feds determine your EFC is $3,000. This is the minimum amount your family is expected to contribute toward the cost of college.

Let's say you get accepted to two colleges, each with different sticker prices:

- Private College A: $56,500 per school year
- Public University B: $21,500 per school year

Let's walk through the three simple steps. First, figure out your financial need.

Step 1: Determine Your Financial Need	
Private College A	**Public University B**
Cost of Attendance: $56,500	Cost of Attendance: $21,500
− Expected Family Contribution: $3,000	− Expected Family Contribution: $3,000
Financial Need: $53,500	Financial Need: $18,500

In Step 2, each college will offer you a financial aid package. Subtract this from your financial need to determine your unmet need.

The strength of your financial aid package depends on how much money the college has to give and how badly they want you. Some private colleges cover 100% of financial need. Public universities tend not to offer as much, but they're also cheaper.

For this example, let's say Private College A will cover 90% of your financial need, and Public University B will cover 50%.

Step 2: Determine Unmet Need	
Private College A Financial Need: $53,500 Financial Aid: $48,150 (90% need met) Unmet Need: $5,350	**Private College A** Financial Need: $18,500 Financial Aid: $9,250 (50% need met) Unmet Need: $9,250

In Step 3, you will add your unmet need and original EFC to find your net price, the amount you will have to cover that year.

Step 3: Determine Net Price	
Private College A Unmet Need: $5,350 EFC: $3,000 Net Price: $8,350	**Private College A** Unmet Need: $9,250 EFC: $3,000 Net Price: $12,250

Private College A, which started with a much higher sticker price, ended up with a lower net price. This doesn't always happen, but I want to make the point that you shouldn't let a school's COA scare you away.

Know that there's more you can do to lower your net price: you can apply for outside and school-specific scholarships, take out additional loans, appeal your financial aid package, and more.

Don't get stuck on the numbers in my illustration, which are fictional. Rather, focus on understanding the key steps and terms, which will empower you to plan ahead and apply to colleges your family will be able to afford. One way to plan ahead is to go through the process I have outlined here with more realistic numbers. Every college is required to provide an online net price calculator, which helps prospective students determine, with reasonable accuracy, if they will be able to afford a given school.

Sources of Financial Aid

"Financial aid" refers to money that helps you pay for college. There are four main sources:

1. Federal government
2. State government
3. Institution (the college itself)
4. Scholarship organizations

Source 1: Federal government

The only way to secure federal student aid is to submit your FAFSA. Learn more at studentaid.ed.gov. The U.S. Department of Education offers federal student aid, which comes in three forms:

1. **Grants** are "gift aid," meaning you don't have to pay them back. They are usually need-based (i.e., for students with financial need). The federal government offers four grant programs; you can learn more at studentaid.ed.gov/sa/types.

2. **Loans** are "self-help aid." Students borrow money from the federal government and must pay it back with interest. (Interest is the price you pay to borrow money.) Whether a federal loan is "subsidized" or "unsubsidized" has to do with its terms for paying interest. In almost all cases, both subsidized and unsubsidized federal loans are kinder to borrowers than private loans are. Try to avoid private loans. There are four main federal loan programs; you can learn more at studentaid.ed.gov/sa/types.

3. **Work-study** programs are another form of self-help aid. They connect students who have financial need to part-time jobs on or around their campuses. You can learn more at studentaid.ed.gov/sa/types.

Source 2: State government

Many states have special programs to distribute student aid, which can come in the form of loans, grants, and scholarships. Examples include Louisiana's Taylor Opportunity Program for Students (TOPS), Georgia's Helping Outstanding Pupils Educationally (HOPE), and California's Cal Grants. Note that you usually have to be an in-state resident to benefit from these and other state programs.

Find out if your state offers financial aid programs and, if so, what the qualifications are for securing state aid. Contact your state agency at www.ed.gov/sgt, review the information on finaid.org/otheraid/state.phtml, speak to your counselor, or call the college's financial aid office.

Filing your FAFSA is essential for securing not only federal but also state student aid. Use the resources above or studentaid.ed.gov/sa/fafsa#deadlines to determine your state's priority deadline for FAFSA completion and to be sure you've completed any other required forms on time.

Source 3: Institutional aid

A college is an institution, so "institutional aid" is just a fancy way of saying financial aid that comes directly from a college. Many people don't realize colleges have their own money, which they distribute to students. The only way to access institutional aid is to complete your FAFSA—and in certain cases, your CSS Profile—on time. There are two forms of institutional aid:

1. **Need-based aid** is granted to a student because they has a financial need. It usually doesn't need to be paid back.

2. **Merit-based aid** also does not typically need to be paid back. It's granted to a student for specific talents or accomplishments: academic, musical, athletic, community service-focused, or another kind. Some colleges will automatically offer merit-based aid to students they accept and really want. Other times colleges will offer school-specific, merit-based scholarships that students must apply for separately. While these school-specific scholarships can be tough to win, I have found that students often overlook them altogether, leaving significant money on the table. Make sure to visit the financial aid webpage of each college you apply to in order to find out which available school-specific awards you can compete for.

Source 4: Scholarship organizations

A "scholarship organization" is a general term for any organization—besides the federal government, state government, or a college—that offers gift aid. There are three main categories of scholarship organizations:

1. **Foundations** donate money to worthy causes—like, for instance, a hardworking student trying to pay for college. You have likely heard of the Bill & Melinda Gates Foundation, the Michael & Susan Dell Foundation, and the Jack Kent Cooke Foundation, but there are literally thousands nationwide. Many foundations support students in particular cities, states, or regions.

2. **Corporations**, like Taco Bell, Dr. Pepper, and Coca Cola, offer scholarships to aspiring college students. Just like foundations, there are thousands of corporations, both large and small. They don't have to be international behemoths like the ones I named. Local, state-wide, and regional corporations are more likely to support students in the places where they operate.

3. **Other scholarship organizations** like churches, nonprofits, sororities, fraternities, recreational clubs, and any group that reserves money for scholarships. These range from local organizations (like Rotary Club and Kiwanis) to large national nonprofits (like NACCP, United Negro College Fund). There are too many to count, and so the number of scholarships is almost endless. Ask club sponsors, your clergyperson, coaches, and high school counselor if they can suggest scholarships that you can apply to.

Complete Your FAFSA

The Free Application for Federal Student Aid (FAFSA) is a free and simple form the federal government uses to determine your Expected Family Contribution (EFC), the minimum amount your family is expected to contribute toward your college education. The federal government will then send your EFC to the colleges you are applying to, which they'll use to determine your financial aid package.

If you take one thing from this chapter, take this: You will not be eligible for federal student aid—or most other forms of financial aid—if you don't complete your FAFSA.

What financial information you report on the FAFSA depends on your dependency status. If you are a dependent student, you will report your and your parents' financial information. If you are an independent student, you will report only your financial information. If you're an independent student and you're married, you will report your and your spouse's information.

The federal government says that an independent student is one of the following: "at least 24 years old, married, a graduate or professional student, a veteran, a member of the armed forces, an orphan, a ward of the court, someone with legal dependents other than a spouse, an emancipated minor, or someone who is either homeless or at risk of becoming homeless."

The FAFSA opens on October 1 of each year. Since financial aid is granted on a first-come, first-served basis, you should aim to file your FAFSA as soon as possible after October 1. This free application leads to free money! It's easier to fill out than it seems, especially if you're prepared. Below is what you need in order to file your FAFSA.

1. **FSA ID:** This is your personal login to access your FAFSA, the myStudentAid mobile app, and other Department of Education websites and financial aid forms. If you are a dependent student, one of your parents (or whoever's financial information you reported) will also need an FSA ID. You cannot create your parent's FSA ID, and they cannot create yours. Get started at www.fsaid.gov.

2. **Key Numbers:**
   - Social Security number (found on your Social Security card)
   - Driver's license number (if you have one)
   - Alien Registration Number (if you are not a U.S. Citizen)

3. **Prior-prior tax records:** This is taxable income dating back two years before you enroll in college (that's why it's called prior-prior). Anyone reporting taxable income will need federal tax information or tax returns, including IRS W-2 information.

   But there's good news! The FAFSA has incorporated a resource called the IRS Data Retrieval Tool (IRS DRT), which allows you to import most of your tax information straight from the IRS into your FAFSA. This saves time and prevents mistakes. You should still have your tax records handy, since the IRS DRT does not input all tax information that the FAFSA requires.

4. **Records of untaxed income:** Untaxed income includes child support received, interest income, and veterans noneducation benefits. Questions about untaxed income may or may not apply to you (and your parents, if you're a dependent student).

5. **Records of assets:** This is any and all information on cash, savings and checking account balances, investments (including stocks, bonds, and real estate—but it does not include the home you live in), and business and farm assets.

6. **List of colleges you are applying to:** Tell the federal government which colleges you want your FAFSA results sent to. You can list up to 10 at a time, but there is a way to add more if you need. See "How to Add Additional Colleges to Your FAFSA and CSS Profiles" at the end of this chapter.

Final notes

- Utilize the worksheet available at studentaid.ed.gov/sa/help/fafsa-worksheet to preview the questions FAFSA will ask you.

- If you are a dependent student, file your FAFSA with your parents.

- If possible, file your FAFSA with a trusted counselor who has experience.

- Set aside a couple hours so you can take your time and do it right.

- Be aware of priority FAFSA deadlines for different colleges and scholarships.

- You must file your FAFSA for every year that you are seeking federal student aid.

Complete Your CSS Profile

What is the CSS Profile?

The CSS Profile is similar to the FAFSA in that colleges use it to assess your family's financial situation and determine your financial aid package. You do not submit the CSS Profile instead of the FAFSA. Never do that. Rather, you submit the CSS Profile *in addition* to the FAFSA if you are applying to colleges or scholarship organizations that require it.

Who requires a CSS Profile?

Visit the College Board for a list of colleges and scholarship organizations that may require the CSS Profile in addition to the FAFSA. There are almost 400 in total.

When should I submit the CSS Profile?

Like the FAFSA, the CSS Profile is available October 1. Find out the priority deadlines from the colleges and scholarship organizations you're applying to, and then make sure you submit your CSS Profile no later than two weeks before their deadline. Many deadlines fall between January 1 and March 31, but it can be as early as November.

Why is there a CSS Profile and a FAFSA?

The FAFSA is primarily used to determine your eligibility for federal student aid (like grants, loans, and work-study). Private colleges, certain state universities, and some foundations use the CSS Profile to take a deeper look at your family's financial situation to determine your eligibility for their institutional financial aid.

Is the CSS Profile free like the FAFSA?

No, but the expense is worth it for the aid you could receive. It costs $25 to fill out and submit the CSS Profile to one school. Every additional school you submit your CSS Profile to will cost $16. If you used an SAT fee waiver, you will be automatically eligible to receive a CSS Profile waiver for up to eight school reports.

What if my parents are not together?

In this case, your "custodial" parent (the parent who has legal custody over you) should fill out the main Profile. Your noncustodial parent may be required to complete a separate noncustodial form.

Completing the CSS Profile
Phase 1: Get prepared

1. **Create a College Board account:** You may already have one from when you took the SAT and/or an SAT II Subject Test. If so, make sure to use the same login.

2. **Gather key financial documents:**
   - Federal tax returns from one and two years prior to when you'll enroll in college
   - W-2 forms and other records of income from one and two years prior to when you'll enroll in college
   - Records of untaxed income from one and two years prior to when you'll enroll in college
   - Current bank statements and mortgage information
   - Records of any stocks, bonds, trusts, and other investments you or your parents have

Phase 2: Fill it out

Below is a broad overview of information the CSS Profile asks for. I recommend you also use the step-by-step instructions The College Board provides each year.

Parent Information

- Basic info: name, date of birth, employment status, level of education, contact information, marital status, etc.

- Household info: basic info about your parents' household, such as number of dependent family members, if any of them are already in college, etc.

- Income and benefits for one and two years before you will enroll in college

- Expected income and benefits for the year you will enroll in college; also report any anticipated increases or decreases from previous year

- Assets: questions about cash, savings, and checking accounts as well as other assets like investments, businesses, farms, real estate, retirement accounts, and educational savings. If your parents own their home, there will be questions about home equity.

- Expenses: including child support payments, educational costs, and medical and dental expenses not covered by insurance

- Noncustodial parent information: if your parents are not together, your custodial parent will complete this section; if that parent is unable to, you will be able to explain why later; in the case of parents not being together, many colleges and scholarship organizations ask for a separate noncustodial parent form.

Student Information

- Basic info: state of legal residence, dependency status, Social Security number, etc.
- Income and benefits from the last two years
- Expected resources for the upcoming school year: total amount of financial aid you will have through family support, outside scholarships, and work. Estimates are fine.
- Assets: checking or savings accounts in your name as well as any investments, including certificates of deposit, savings bonds, stocks, or real estate that you own
- Expenses for last year: if you are an independent student, you should report child support that you or your spouse paid to former spouse(s) as well as any medical and dental expenses you had last year that weren't covered by insurance
- Dependent family member listing: questions about dependent members of your household other than your parents

Explanations/Special Circumstances

This is an optional, open-response section you can use to:

- Explain anything unusual in your application.
- Explain special circumstances not reflected in your application that will affect your family's ability to pay for college (unusually high medical bills, loss of employment, natural disaster, etc.).
- Report outside scholarships you've already received.
- Complete answers from previous sections where more room was needed.

Supplemental Information

You will only see this section if one or more of the colleges or scholarship organizations to which you're applying require more information.

Once you've submitted the CSS Profile, you'll have a chance to confirm which colleges and scholarship organizations will receive it. You will also have a chance to review your responses and make corrections if necessary. Save the acknowledgement of submission for your records.

Understanding Financial Aid Award Letters

After you've been accepted to a college, that school's financial aid office will send you a financial aid award letter. This letter will break down the different kinds and amounts of financial aid the college is offering you. The key word is "offering." You don't have to accept the entire award package. An award letter can come in the mail, online, and sometimes, both.

The way information is presented on award letters will vary from college to college. Some award letters are very clear, while others have to be deciphered like a cave drawing. In order to make the smartest financial decision, you need to find the following information:

* Cost of attendance (tuition, room and board, books, personal expenses, travel)

* Grants (federal, state, and/or institutional)

* Scholarships (federal, state, and/or institutional)

* Work-study

* Loans

* Expected Family Contribution (EFC)

It's possible that some of this information won't be in the letter your college sends you. In that case, you'll have to call up or email the financial aid office to find out. Sometimes their website will cover this information, even if their letter doesn't.

Many colleges—nearly 3,000, in fact—use something called the Financial Aid Shopping Sheet as a template for award letters. The Shopping Sheet was intended to show clarity and consistency in how schools present their financial aid offers to students. Take a look on the next page to see what the Shopping Sheet looks like.

College and student info

Student cost of attendance before grants and scholarships

Total amount of federal, state, institutional grants, and scholarships

Net price (what you actually have to pay) after gift aid

Aid awarded by school through work-study

School-recommended federal loan amounts and types

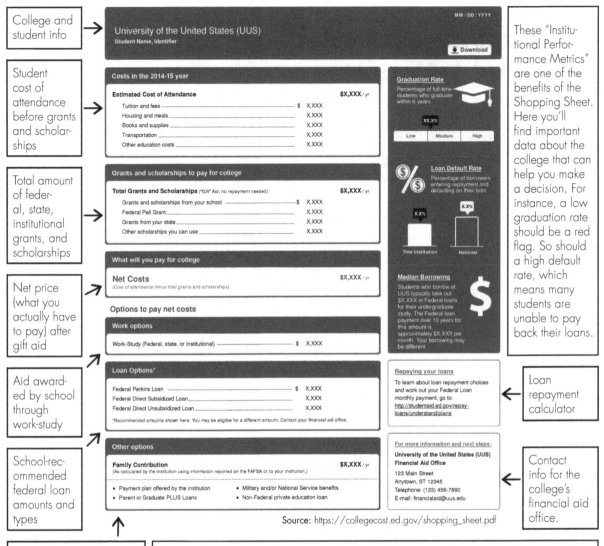

MM / DD / YYYY

University of the United States (UUS)
Student Name, Identifier

⬇ Download

Costs in the 2014-15 year

Estimated Cost of Attendance   **$X,XXX** / yr

Tuition and fees ——————— $ X,XXX
Housing and meals _____ X,XXX
Books and supplies _____ X,XXX
Transportation _____ X,XXX
Other education costs _____ X,XXX

Grants and scholarships to pay for college

Total Grants and Scholarships ("Gift" Aid; no repayment needed)   **$X,XXX** / yr

Grants and scholarships from your school ——— $ X,XXX
Federal Pell Grant _____ X,XXX
Grants from your state _____ X,XXX
Other scholarships you can use ___ X,XXX

What will you pay for college

Net Costs   **$X,XXX** / yr
(Cost of attendance minus total grants and scholarships)

Options to pay net costs

Work options

Work-Study (Federal, state, or institutional) ——— $ X,XXX

Loan Options*

Federal Perkins Loan ——————— $ X,XXX
Federal Direct Subsidized Loan_____ X,XXX
Federal Direct Unsubsidized Loan_____ X,XXX

*Recommended amounts shown here. You may be eligible for a different amount. Contact your financial aid office.

Other options

Family Contribution   **$X,XXX** / yr
(As calculated by the institution using information reported on the FAFSA or to your institution.)

• Payment plan offered by the institution   • Military and/or National Service benefits
• Parent or Graduate PLUS Loans   • Non-Federal private education loan

Graduation Rate
Percentage of full-time students who graduate within 6 years

XX.X%

Low   Medium   High

Loan Default Rate
Percentage of borrowers entering repayment and defaulting on their loan

X.X%   X.X%

This institution   National

Median Borrowing
Students who borrow at UUS typically take out $X,XXX in Federal loans for their undergraduate study. The Federal loan payment over 10 years for this amount is approximately $X,XXX per month. Your borrowing may be different.

Repaying your loans
To learn about loan repayment choices and work out your Federal Loan monthly payment, go to:
http://studentaid.ed.gov/repay-loans/understand/plans

For more information and next steps:
University of the United States (UUS)
Financial Aid Office
123 Main Street
Anytown, ST 12345
Telephone: (123) 456-7890
E-mail: financialaid@uus.edu

Source: https://collegecost.ed.gov/shopping_sheet.pdf

These "Institutional Performance Metrics" are one of the benefits of the Shopping Sheet. Here you'll find important data about the college that can help you make a decision. For instance, a low graduation rate should be a red flag. So should a high default rate, which means many students are unable to pay back their loans.

Loan repayment calculator

Contact info for the college's financial aid office.

Your college uses this space to make recommendations for other ways to cover your net costs. This includes your family's contribution (EFC), taking out other loans, and looking into federal benefits that can lead to more aid.

Your college may use this space on the bottom to write you a customized message about your award letter.

Remember: How financial aid is presented will vary from college to college. Many colleges use the Shopping Sheet, which is nice and simple. But some don't. No matter what the format is, you need to read each of your award letters carefully in order to fully understand your financial aid offer. The more carefully you read and the more questions you ask, the more likely you will be to understand exactly how much each college will cost you and your family.

Great External Resource:
To see examples of different kinds of financial aid award letters, visit bigfuture.collegeboard.org/get-started/for- parents/webinar-its-time- comparing-financial-aid- award-letters.

Comparing Financial Aid Award Letters

Before we get into how to compare award letters, a few reminders:

- The offer may not be final: It's possible the financial aid office is missing information from you, in which case the award package is considered "tentative" or "provisional." The award letter will say so and provide steps to follow.

- Reporting outside scholarships: Each college has its own rules on reporting outside scholarships. You need to follow them. The amount you earn in outside scholarships may affect the amount of financial aid the college offers you.

- The key word is "offer": An award package is an offer; it's not set in stone. You can accept it as is, reject all or part of it, or request for it to be changed by writing an appeal.

- Compare colleges, too: Comparing award letters is about money, but choosing a college is about more than cost. Don't forget the features other than cost that attracted you to these schools in the first place.

How to Compare Financial Aid Award Letters

Some financial aid award letters will be easy to understand; others won't. Use the "Award Comparison Spreadsheet" at the end of this chapter to compare the exact same costs at each school. If your award letter doesn't have this information, you will need to contact the financial aid office to find out these numbers. This is what you need in order to effectively compare schools:

Cost of attendance:

Tuition, fees, and room & board are hard costs that can be found on a college's website. Books, supplies, travel, and personal expenses vary from person to person. Your award letter might estimate these costs, but you should think about what's realistic for you.

Total amount of gift aid:

- Grants and scholarships (federal, state, and institutional)
- Other (scholarships from outside sources; e.g., Gates Scholarship)

Total amount of self-help aid:

- Loans
    - o Federal Direct Loans (subsidized and unsubsidized Stafford loans)
    - o Federal Perkins Loans
    - o Other student loans

- Income from work
    - o Federal work-study
    - o Other job offer(s)

There are several online tools helpful for financial aid comparisons. I recommend The College Board's award comparison calculator, which aligns with our "Award Comparison Spreadsheet." You can view it here: <u>bigfuture.collegeboard.org/pay-for-college/financial-aid-awards/compare-aid-calculator</u>.

Writing out all the above amounts from every school will give you a good starting point for understanding what each college will cost you and your family. To make a thorough comparison, you'll need to compare both the quantity and quality of your financial aid. In other words, you need to examine the types and amounts of loans, work-study, and gift aid each school has offered you.

Comparing Loan Offers

If you notice that your family's share of costs is very low for one college, look more closely. Sometimes this signals that a high percentage of your financial aid is coming from loans. Make sure you know if you can afford to take out the amount in loans that each college is offering.

The College Board provides a great loan comparison tool found at <u>bigfuture.collegeboard.org/pay-for-college/loans/student-loan-comparison-calculator</u>. Like their awards comparison calculator, this calculator allows you to plug in the different types and amounts of loans each college is offering. The calculator will spit out results showing the total amount you will end up having to repay as well as your monthly payment responsibilities in each case.

Use the "Loan Comparison Spreadsheet" at the end of this chapter to track results from each college side by side and take a hard look at the results. Be realistic about what you and your family can afford, now and in the long run. Remember that a loan offer is just that: an offer. You do not have to accept the full amount of any loan being offered, especially if you can find other sources of funds for college.

If you are confused about loan terms, reach out to the college's financial aid office. Here are some questions to ask:

- Are there any fees that will reduce the amount I actually receive?

- Is the interest rate paid by the government while I'm in school? Or is it deferred and added to the loan amount?

- When do I start repayment?

- How much will I owe by the time I graduate?

- How much is my monthly bill going to be when I graduate?

- Will my loan increase after my first year and, if so, by how much?

- Are there any favorable repayment programs, such as deferment for graduate school, forgiveness for particular professions, or income-contingent repayment?

Comparing Work-Study

Work-study can be another source of income for you, but it will affect your day-to-day college life. This is why it's important to compare the different work-study options presented in your award letters. Here are some good questions to ask:

- Do I have a guaranteed job, or do I have to find one?

- How are jobs assigned?

- How many hours per week will I be expected to work?

- What is the hourly wage?

- How often will I be paid?

- Do I get paid regularly, or can my student account be credited?

Comparing Gift Aid

Even though gift aid is free money, it's important that you understand what, if any, strings are attached to it. For example, certain scholarships require that you maintain a certain GPA. Other scholarships require that you pursue certain majors. You want to know what these strings are before you accept a college's admission.

When comparing different gift aid offers, here are some questions to ask:

- Are there any circumstances under which I could lose this gift aid?

- Is there a minimum GPA or some other requirement I have to meet?

- Will I receive the same amount of gift aid each year I'm in college?

- What happens to my award if I win an outside scholarship during college?

- Can the aid be increased if my family experiences financial troubles?

- How, if at all, does college enrollment of a sibling impact my award?

When to Appeal Your Financial Aid Offer

"Appealing" a financial aid award offer is a fancy way of saying "ask the college for more money." Different colleges have different policies for and attitudes about appeals. Below are some scenarios in which an appeal might result in more aid. The first two are your best shots. The second two scenarios may or may not work; as always, it depends on the college.

1. **A major life change for you and/or your family:**
   - Death
   - Disability or illness
   - Divorce, separation, or remarriage
   - Birth of a sibling
   - Care for an elderly parent

2. **Significant financial changes:**
   - Unemployment or decreased income
   - Moved or sold home
   - Tuition for private school for a sibling/dependent
   - Increase in child care expenses
   - Siblings/dependents attending college
   - Changes in number of dependents in household

3. **Other school(s) offered you more:** If School A offers more financial aid than School B, you could try to leverage School A's offer to get more money out of School B. Not every school will play this game, and whether or not School B shows you the money will depend on how much they want you.

4. **Academic merit:** You can make an appeal on the basis of a new and improved SAT/ACT score or some other form of impressive academic growth. This is not a surefire strategy, but it can't hurt to try.

How to File an Appeal

Your college will have a specific process for appealing. The steps may be laid out in your award letter, or you may have to call the financial aid office to find out. On the next page, you will find a sample appeal letter. Not every college will require one, but many will.

Tips for Successful Appeals

- **Act fast:** You can't control the timing of circumstances that warrant an appeal. Just try to appeal your offers as soon as possible after you receive them. Remember that aid is disbursed on a first-come, first-served basis and that other students may be in a similar position as you.

- **Get documentation:** Be prepared to provide official documentation that supports your reason(s) for requesting an appeal. For example, if your mother or father becomes unemployed, you could secure a letter from their former employer.

- **Don't challenge the college:** No matter the scenario, don't challenge the financial aid officer by exclaiming, "If you can't give me more aid, I'm not coming!" If you're appealing, it's because you want to attend. Express your sincere interest, and explain that cost is the only thing standing in your way.

- **Be polite and respectful:** You'll catch more bees with honey than vinegar.

As long as you're not a jerk about it, you have nothing to lose but time by appealing. When you appeal, you are not whining or complaining. You are self-advocating, a skill critical to success in college and beyond. You are simply asking for what you need. Don't be ashamed of that. In fact, get really good at it.

Your Name
Street Address
City, State, Zip

Office of Financial Aid
Future Success University
1234 College Drive
Baton Rouge, Louisiana 70810

(Today's date)

To the Office of Financial Aid

My name is _____ and I was recently accepted to Future Success University for the fall of 2015. I am writing to respectfully request consideration of appeal for my financial aid award package.

I am very excited about the opportunity to attend FSU and am grateful for the financial aid package the University has offered me thus far. However, I am still facing a large financial gap that, in spite of the school's generosity, would make attending impossible for me.

My three younger brothers and I live with my mother who is a single parent. Though we always knew paying for college would be challenging, we made plans to figure it out. However, one month ago, my mother un-expectedly lost her job as a school bus driver. I have attached a formal letter from her manager documenting the layoff.

Now, our primary source of income is my mother's unemployment benefits. I have secured a part-time job at American Eagle, but I have to put any income I earn toward our family's daily expenses and bills. I haven't met my father nor do I know where he lives, and thus I can't ask him for financial support. Suffice to say, the five of us are struggling to make ends meet.

My expectation is that my mother will regain employment in the near future, and that soon we will not be in such a desperate financial situation. However, in the meantime, I am writing with the hope that you will take these new circumstances into consideration as you review my financial aid package for the coming school year.

Future Success University has been my dream school for the last four years. This school is a perfect fit for me academically and socially, and I feel confident that I would contribute to the campus community.

Thank you so much for taking time to read this letter and for considering my request. Please contact me if you would like any additional information.

Sincerely,

Your Name
Phone Number
Email Address

What You Need to Know About Accepting Loans

Remember: when it comes to accepting financial aid, you want free money first (grants and scholarships), then earned money (work-study), and finally, borrowed money (loans). For most students, taking out loans is unavoidable. If you're one of those students, here's some advice about accepting loans.

DISCLAIMER: DON'T DO THIS ALONE!

Seek the support of a parent, mentor, teacher, counselor, financial aid officer, or other adult who has experience with this process and knows how to make responsible borrowing choices.

Which loans should you accept?

Always accept loans with the most favorable terms and conditions. Usually this means federal and state loans. If you are considering taking out a private loan, remember that they usually have less favorable terms and conditions and may end up costing you more money in the long run. If you see private or commercial loans in your award letter, ask the financial aid office why this type of loan was included and learn the terms—if the terms aren't favorable, reject the private loan.

Do you have to accept a college's entire loan offer?

Absolutely not! In fact, you should never borrow more than you need. In your award letter, the school will tell you what steps to take for rejecting loans.

How do you tell the school what you're accepting?

Any loan offered on your award letter will come with instructions on how to accept or decline the offer. Read your award letter carefully and follow the school's financial aid instructions. Ultimately your school's financial aid office will lead you to www.studentloans.gov, where you will have to sign the Master Promissory Note (MPN), a contract between you and the federal government that outlines the terms and conditions of the loan. By signing the MPN, you are promising to pay back the loan. After signing the MPN, first-time borrowers will have to go through entrance counseling, an online training to help you manage your college expenses and better understand your loan responsibilities.

When and how will you receive your loan money?

As always, it depends on the school. Different schools have different schedules and methods of disbursement. Generally, you will receive aid either at least once per term (semester, trimester, or quarter) or twice per academic year. Once your school receives federal funds, it will either transfer your loan money to your school account, give you money directly, or a combination of both.

What is a loan servicer?

The federal government lends you money, and the loan servicer makes sure you pay it back. A loan servicer is a middleman company that handles administration of your loan, including billing, helping you select a repayment plan, working with you on loan consolidation, and managing any other loan-related actions.

Who will your loan servicer be?

Your loan servicer will be one of the eleven loan servicing companies the federal government has approved. The federal government will assign one to you.

When and how will I hear from my loan servicer?

Your loan servicer will usually contact you via email after you've received your first disbursement. Throughout college, your loan servicer will contact you periodically, usually via email, with important information and action steps. As you near the end of college, your loan servicer will contact you to help you make decisions about how you will repay your loan(s) after graduation.

When do I need to contact my school, and when do I need to contact my loan servicer?

If your loan is for the current or upcoming school year, contact your school's financial aid office directly for information about:

- loan status
- loan cancellation within 120 days of disbursement
- loan disbursement amounts and timing

While you're in college, contact your loan servicer when you:

- change your name, address, or phone number
- graduate
- drop below half-time enrollment
- stop going to school

- transfer to another school
- want to get educated about loan repayment and/or consolidation

If you're no longer in school, contact your loan servicer when you:

- change your name, address, or phone number
- need help making your loan payment
- have a question about your bill
- have other questions about your student loan

What You Need to Know About Scholarships

Gift aid is money you don't have to pay back. A scholarship is a form of gift aid you usually have to complete a separate application for.

Scholarships are awesome, but in my experience, they're also dangerous. That's because they can be a major waste of time. Each year a very small minority of high-performing students will earn full or major scholarships, and the majority will not be able to pay for college by securing a series of smaller ones. Rather, most students will pay for college through a combination of federal, state, and institutional aid, with a fortunate few securing outside scholarships to reduce their expenses.

I'm not telling you not to apply for scholarships. I am telling you not to depend on them and to be smart about how you spend your limited time. The best use of your time is to focus on the Big Five: GPA, SAT/ACT, essays, involvement, and recommendation letters. A strong Big Five will set you up to maximize state and institutional gift aid and make you more competitive when it's time to apply for outside scholarships.

There are two scenarios where it makes sense to apply for a scholarship:

1. It's a good match—meaning you're eligible and would be competitive—and you're prepared to dedicate the time and energy necessary to do a great job.

2. Applying requires little time and effort, so you have nothing to lose.

Since the second scenario is self-explanatory and happens rarely, let's focus on the first one. How do you find scholarships that will be good matches for you?

One way is to use scholarship-matching sites, some of which are listed below. These sites take your information—GPA, SAT/ACT, gender identity, ethnicity, religious tradition, etc.—and generate a list of possible scholarship opportunities.

A second way, and my recommendation, is to conduct your own deep, online research using keywords to focus your searches. The "Scholarship Match Worksheet" at the end of this chapter should help you come up with some of these keywords.

Scholarship websites:

- fastweb.com
- scholarships.com
- collegeboard.org
- collegexpress.com
- myscholly.com
- niche.com
- moolahspot.com
- cappex.com
- unigo.com
- chegg.com

Eleven Scholar Tips for Scholarships

1. **Don't overlook school-specific scholarships:** Visit the financial aid websites of the colleges you apply to and see which scholarship opportunities they offer to incoming freshmen. Get on this ASAP so you don't miss early deadlines.

2. **Keep track of deadlines and requirements:** Use an Excel or Google spreadsheet to stay organized about what is due when.

3. **Search near you:** Don't just search nationally. There are scholarship organizations in your backyard. Find out which local businesses, Greek organizations, places of worship, and civic and professional groups offer scholarships. If you can't find what you need on their websites, call them. Split the work with a friend so you can both benefit.

4. **Search what you know:** Google, Nike, Coca Cola, Taco Bell, Burger King, State Farm. Heard of these? Major brand name companies usually offer scholarships. I can't promise they will be a good match for you, but it's worth looking.

5. **Look for state government scholarships:** Use the links I shared earlier in this chapter, under "Sources of Financial Aid," to determine whether your state's government offers special scholarships, usually awarded to students who attend in-state colleges.

6. **Check out military scholarships:** A massive amount of funding is available to students who intend to become military officers either by attending U.S. service academies or participating in ROTC. Be clear on their requirements.

7. **Avoid time-consuming marketing ploys:** Some corporations offer scholarships that require applicants to collect votes or "likes" on social media. Stay away from these unless your goal is to promote the company for no reward.

8. **Avoid scholarship scams:** Stay away from scholarships that require payment of any kind or generally seem too good to be true.

9. **Be aware of strings attached:** Before applying for a scholarship, know what will be required of you to keep it. For instance, most military scholarships obligate you to serve in the military after college. Other programs require that you maintain a certain GPA or participate in a sport or club.

10. **Talk to teachers and counselors:** It's quite possible they've had past students win big awards and never mentioned anything. It never hurts to ask.

11. **Search early:** If you can enter senior year with a strong scholarship list and handful of solid essays, you'll have more success with scholarships.

Reporting Outside Scholarships

Different colleges have different rules on reporting outside scholarships, and you need to follow them. What you earn in outside scholarships may affect the amount of financial aid a college offers you. Some schools might decrease your gift aid so they can offer other students more, but some will decrease your loans, which is great. Other times, your aid may be unaffected. In any case, make sure you follow each college's policies on reporting outside scholarships.

Examples of Major Scholarships

*Scholarships with an * are school-specific awards*

Name	Who is this for?
Gates Scholarships	Low-income, minority students with strong academic, leadership, and community service records.
QuestBridge	High-achieving, low-income high school juniors and seniors.
Morehead-Cain* (UNC Chapel Hill)	Outstanding applicants to the University of North Carolina at Chapel Hill.
Levin Scholarship* (UNC Charlotte)	Outstanding applicants to the University of North Carolina-Charlotte with strong community service records.

Ron Brown Scholarships	African-American high school seniors with strong academic and leadership records.
Jack Kent Cooke Scholarships	Students with exceptional academic ability and achievement, financial need, persistence, a desire to help others, and leadership.
Jefferson Scholars Program* (University of Virginia)	Applicants to the University of Virginia with extraordinary intellectual range and depth who possess the highest qualities of leadership, scholarship, and citizenship.
Jackie Robinson Scholarship	Minority students attending four-year colleges with a minimum ACT of 21.
Buick Achievers Scholarships	High-achieving students who plan to pursue degrees and careers in engineering.
Bonner Scholarship	High-achieving students with strong community service records.

In Summary...

- Read your financial aid award letter *carefully* so you can be sure what kind of financial aid the school is offering to you.

- Loans can be useful, but you have to pay them back with interest.

- Grants are better, but some come with strings attached (or it's not free money after all).

- Work-study is a great way to develop work experience while earning money to pay off college expenses.

- Fill out your FAFSA! This is the only way you will qualify for school, state, or government financial aid. Submit your FAFSA as close to October 1 as you can.

- Use the worksheets on the next several pages to keep on track and make your best school choice with confidence. You can also access these online: www.masteryprep.com/cpb-resources. Password is *CollegeSuccess*.

Scholarship Reference Guide

There are four main sources of money for college besides family support or your own income:

1. Federal government aid (grants, loans, work-study)

How? File your FAFSA as early as possible after October 1

CRITICAL: Every college you apply to needs your FAFSA. Refer to "How to Add Additional Colleges to Your FAFSA and CSS Profiles."

2. State government aid (varies by state—Louisiana TOPS, Georgia HOPE, etc.)

How? www.nasfaa.org/state_financial_aid_programs

3. Institutional aid (money directly from a college's bank account)

How? Get accepted by the school

How? Apply for school-specific scholarships that require a separate application

CRITICAL: You'll get precisely zero institutional aid if your school requires the CSS Profile and you don't complete and send it to that school. To find out if your college requires the CSS Profile, visit: profile.collegeboard.org/profile/ppi/participatingInstitutions.aspx

CRITICAL: You must send your CSS Profile to every college you apply to that requires it. Refer to "How to Add Additional Colleges to Your FAFSA and CSS Profiles."

4. Outside scholarships (awards from foundations, corporations, and other scholarship organizations)

How? Search for them online and submit strong applications, usually with essays

What's the deal with school-specific scholarships?

- These are scholarships colleges give out to accepted students straight from their bank account.
- Sometimes you will be considered for them just by applying to the college.
- Other times you have to apply for school-specific scholarships separately. They can be found on a college's financial aid webpage, which usually isn't too hard to find.

Example: www.scholarships.ua.edu

Not all financial aid pages are equally easy to find. Be patient and persistent.

How do I know if it's worth it to apply for a scholarship?

There are two scenarios:

1. It's a good match—meaning you're eligible and would be competitive—and you're prepared to dedicate the time and energy necessary to do a great job.
2. Applying requires little time and effort, so you have nothing to lose.

Where else can I find scholarships?

This list is helpful but not exhaustive. It's up to you to do the research!

Scholarship Search Engines	National Scholarship Resources	Other
www.worldscholarshipforum.com www.fastweb.com www.scholarships.com www.collegenet.com www.collegeboard.org www.collegeexpress.com www.myscholly.com www.niche.com www.moolahspot.com www.cappex.com www.unigo.com www.chegg.com www.raise.me	United Negro College Fund Gates Foundation Dell Foundation Jack Kent Cooke Foundation Jackie Robinson Scholarship Taco Bell Foundation The Brown Foundation Buick Achievers Scholarship **Good Ol' Google** If you use Google to search for scholarships, you need two things: 1. **Specific search terms:** use the "Scholarship Match Worksheet" to narrow your search. 2. **Persistence:** If you give up easily, you'll be overwhelmed by Google search results.	• Ask your counselor • Ask if parents' employers offer scholarships • Call local businesses or visit their websites (if they have no scholarships, ask under what circumstances they would create one) • Search brands you know (e.g., Coca Cola, Google, Nike, Taco Bell, etc.)

Warnings
1. **Avoid time-consuming marketing ploys:** Some corporations offer scholarships that require applicants to collect votes or "likes" on social media. Stay away from these unless your goal is to promote the company for no reward.
2. **Avoid scholarship scams:** Stay away from scholarships that require payment of any kind or generally seem too good to be true.
3 **Be aware of strings attached:** Before applying for a scholarship, know what will be required of you to keep it. For instance, most military scholarships obligate you to serve in the military after college. Other programs require that you maintain a certain GPA or participate in a sport or club.

How to Add Additional Colleges to Your FAFSA and CSS Profiles

FAFSA: How to Add Additional Colleges

You can send your FAFSA to up to 10 colleges at one time. If you apply to more than 10 colleges, follow the steps below to submit your FAFSA to additional schools:

1. After your FAFSA has been processed (meaning that you have received an email saying it has been processed, typically within about 48 hours of completion), go to www.fafsa.ed.gov.
2. Click "LOG IN".
3. Click "I am the student," then enter your FSA ID username and password.
4. Click "Next".
5. Click "Make FAFSA Corrections".
6. Go to the Schools tab.
7. Remove schools that you have already submitted your FAFSA to.
   - These schools will still receive your FAFSA information.
   - Remove the same number of schools that you need to add (if you need to add an additional 10 schools, remove all the schools you currently have listed).
8. Add the new schools.
9. Go to the signature page and sign your FAFSA again.
10. Submit your FAFSA.
11. You will receive an email immediately.
    - Note: this is *not* the email that states your FAFSA has been processed.
12. You will receive an email (typically within 48 hours) that your changes have been processed.
13. If necessary, you may repeat these steps to add more schools.

CSS Profile: How to Add Additional Colleges

You may add additional colleges to your CSS Profile at any time. Follow these steps:

1. Log into your CSS Profile.
2. Click "Add a College or Program" on your dashboard.
3. You will be charged $16 for each college you add unless you received a waiver when you first completed your profile.

Scholarship Match Worksheet

Basic Info

Gender: _____

Minority status (e.g., African American, Native American): _____

Nationality (e.g., Israeli, Chinese): _____

City of residence: _____

State of residence: _____

Academics

GPA: _____

ACT/SAT: _____

Class rank: _____

Future Plans

Possible major(s): _____

Possible career(s): _____

Special Qualifications

Learning or physical disability: _____

Intention to serve in the military: _____

Family member serves/served in the military: _____

Connections

Local organizations: _____

Local companies: _____

Other

Special passions: _____

Special talents: _____

Outstanding leadership: _____

Outstanding community service: _____

Languages spoken (besides English): _____

Obscure interests or abilities: _____

Other distinguishing factors: _____

Scholarship Tracker

	Put "N/A" if an item doesn't apply to you.	Scholarship 1	Scholarship 2	Scholarship 3	Scholarship 4
Overview	Award amount				
	Requirements to keep award				
	Application deadline				
	Notification date				
	Website				
	Username & password				
Eligibility	Mininum GPA				
	Mininum ACT/SAT				
	Ethnic/minority/religious/etc.				
	Income qualifications				
	Major or career interest				
	Place of residence				
	Military				
	Other				
Requirements	Online application				
	Essays				
	Test scores (ACT, SAT, PSAT, etc.)				
	Art submission				
	Official transcript				
	FAFSA				
	CSS PROFILE				
	Other 1				
	Other 2				
Recs	Recommender(s)				
	Date requested				
	Date submitted				
Submission	Complete final review?				
	Submission instructions (online, mail, etc.)				
	Paid application fee?				
	Date/time of confirmation of submission				
	Sent thank-you notes?				

Award Comparison Spreadsheet

		College 1	College 2	College 3	College 4
	Hard Costs				
Cost of Attendance	Tution				
	Fees				
	Room & board				
	Soft Costs				
	Books & supplies				
	Travel				
	Personal expenses				
	Gift Aid				
Financial Aid	Federal Pell Grant				
	Federal SEOG Grant				
	State grants & scholarships				
	Instiutional grants & scholarships				
	Other grants & scholarships				
	Self-Help Aid				
	Federal Stafford Loan - Subsidized				
	Federal Stafford Loan - Unsubsidized				
	Federal Perkins Loan				
	Other student loans				
	Federal work-study				
	Other job offer				
	Costs				
Results	Total cost of attendance				
	Family share of costs				
	Financial Aid				
	Total financial aid				
	% of award that is gift aid				
	% of award that is loans				
	% of award that is work-study or job				

Loan Comparison Tracker

	College 1	College 2	College 3	College 4
Federal Direct Stafford Loan - Subsidized				
Monthly payment per $1,000				
Total cost per $1,000				
Monthly payment				
Total Amount				
Federal Direct Stafford Loan - Unsubsidized				
Monthly payment per $1,000				
Total cost per $1,000				
Monthly payment				
Total Amount				
Federal PLUS Loan				
Monthly payment per $1,000				
Total cost per $1,000				
Monthly payment				
Total Amount				
Alternative Loans				
Monthly payment per $1,000				
Total cost per $1,000				
Monthly payment				
Total Amount				

Net Price Comparison Spreadsheet

	College 1	College 2	College 3	College 4
Financial aid priority deadline				
Financial aid regular deadline				
Forms required (CSS/FAFSA)				
Cost of Attendance				
Tuition & fees				
Room & board				
Books & supplies				
Travel				
Personal expenses				
Estimated Total Cost of Attendance				
Gift Aid				
Grants & scholarships				
Other gift aid				
Estimated Total Gift Aid				
Estimated Net Price before Self-Help Aid (*Estimated Total Cost of Attendance* minus *Estimated Total Gift Aid*)				
Self-Help Aid				
Federal Stafford Loans				
Federal Perkins Loans				
Other student or parent loans				
Work-study/job offer				
Estimated Total Self-Help Aid				
Estimated Remaining Cost (*Estimated Net Price* minus *Estimated Total Self-Help Aid*)				

Glossary

A

abruptly
suddenly, unexpectedly

administer
manage; be responsible fo running

admission
accepted by an institution or school for enrollment

advancement
promotion to a higher job position

advent
coming into use

affiliated
officially attached or connected to an organization

aimless
without purpose or direction

align
match or fit together

alternative
another option or choice

analyze
study; examine

articulate
express an idea or feeling clearly

aspect
a particular feature or part

aspiration
hope or ambition of achieving something

asset
a useful, valuable thing or person

attainment
accomplishment

attempt

try to achieve or complete something

authentic

genuine, the real deal

avid

eager and enthusiastic

avoidable

able to be prevented

B

barrier

an obstacle that prevents movement or access

bind

put under an obligation; require commitment

bypass

to go past or around

C

cater

provide what's needed or required

causally

one thing causing another

caveat

an exception to the rule

charge

demand or rule

cohort

a group of people

collaborate

work together on the same task or project

commonly

generally or frequently

compelling

powerfully irresistible; drawing attention or interest

compilation

a gathering of separate items into one

component

one part of a larger whole

composite

made up of various parts

comprehension

the act of understanding something

comprise

consist, made up of something

confer

to give something (like a college degree) to someone

confidentiality

keeping secret or private information

consider

think carefully about something, typically before making a decision

considerable

large in size, amount, or extent

consistently

on every occasion

constitute

make up part of a whole

contribution

a part played by someone to bring about a result

converted

to convince or persuade

criteria

standard used to judge something

critical

extremely important

D

debt

money that is due or needs to be paid

declaring a major

making known to a college the degree program a student will follow

deduct

subtract

de-emphasize

reduce the importance of something

demographic

a specific part of a population

demonstrate

proving a fact with explanation and evidence

differentiate

make or become different

dire

extremely serious or urgent

disclose

to make something known or seen

discount

dismiss something because it is not worthy of consideration

discriminatory

showing prejudice on the basis of race, age, sex, etc.

distinguish

point out a difference

diverse

showing great variety

E

drawback
a disadvantage or problem

eagerness
enthusiasm to do something

effective
succesful; creating a result that's desired

elsewhere
some other place

embrace
welcome, support

emphasize
give special importance to something

enable
allow

enrich
improve the quality or value

ensure
make certain

equipped
prepared for a particular situation

equivalent
equal in value

especially
to a great extent; very much

evaluate
judge, grade, assess

everyday

daily, normal.

(Note: many people confuse *everyday* and *every day*. Use the single word when you're describing a noun, and use the two words when you're describing a verb.)

exception

does not follow a rule

exorbitant

unreasonably high

expound

explain in detail

expressly

in a clear and detailed manner

extensive

invovled, detailed

extent

degree or scale

F

facilitate

make an action or process easier

factors

a fact or circumstance that contributes to a result

fatal

leading to failure or disaster

feedback

information about reactions to a product, a person's performance, etc.

flaunt

display something in a showy way

frequently

often, regularly

fulfill
complete; achieve

full-salaried
a full-time employee who is paid a fixed (set) amount of money

G

generate
to create or produce

generic
common, not special or different from others

gradually
slowly

granular
finely detailed

H

honorable
worthy of respect

hub
center of activity; focal point

humanize
to give something a human character

I

identify
assign identity to something

ilicit
not proper or acceptable

implore
beg earnestly

impression
an opinion or feeling about someone or something

imperfect

not perfect; faulty or incomplete

inanimate

not alive, lifeless

inauthentic

not genuine; without sincerity

inform

give facts or information

income-contingent repayment

an arrangement to pay back debt; the monthly amount to repay depends on the debtor's income

incur

to cause something to happen to oneself

independent

able to do something by yourself

indicator

a specific measurement

ineffective

failure to create the desired result

inevitably

certain to happen; unavoidable

influence

being able to have an effect on character, behavior, or a situation

initiative

program

inject

add

intentional

deliberate, done on purpose

interaction
direct communication or involvement

inverse
opposite

invested
involved, interested

investment
paying money for a profit or material result (like a college degree)

itinerary
a planned schedule or agenda

L

launchpad
something that sets a particular activity into motion

legitimate
real, lawful

liability
risk, putting something or someone at a disadvantage

M

maintain
to keep up

manageable
easily controlled, managed, or accomplished

meaningful
having a serious, important, or useful purpose

mentor
an experienced and trusted adviser

method
systematic planning or action

minimum
the least amount possible or required

mirror
imitate or reflect

model
a pattern that can be imitated

montage
small pieces of stories loosely strung together

movement
a change or development

multitude
a large number or amount

myriad
a countless or extremely great number

N

navigate
to steer in a certain direction

notable
worthy of attention

novice
someone who is inexperienced or new to a situation

numerous
many; great in number

O

obtain
to achieve or secure something

occupational
relating to a job or profession

ongoing
continuing

P

on par
as good as or equal to

outstretched
extended or stretched out

overwhelmed
having too much going on

pace
speed

pandering
flattering excessively

pension
regular payment made to a person after he or she has retired from a profession

persist
continue something

perspective
point of view

pique
to stimulate interest or curiosity

polished
improved or refined

portfolio
a selection of work (such as drawings, photographs, etc.) collected over a period of time

possess
to own or have

preoccupied
distracted, obsessed with

prescribed
decided on in advance

prevent

to keep something from happening

primary

having the first place; most important

proactive

creating or controlling a situation by causing something to happen instead of reacting to a situation after it has happened.

proficiency

a high degree of skill or expertise

progress

forward movement toward a destination

promotion

to move forward professionally

prospective

likely to happen at a future date

prosperous

wealthy and successful

pursue

following a path or route

pursuing

following enthusiastically

qualitative

measuring by a characteristic or by comparing to similar objects

quantifiable

able to be measured or counted

quantitative

measured by the quantity of something rather than its quality

Q

R

ravaged
severely damaged; devastated

readiness
state of being ready for something

record
set down in writing for later reference

redundant
no longer needed or useful; repetitive

refer
mention or allude to

reflective
thoughtful

regress
return to a less developed state

reliable
dependable; trustworthy

remiss
not paying attention; not taking care of a responsibility

repertoire
a compilation of skills or ability; a portfolio

repetitive
repeating over and over

respite
a short period of rest or relief from a difficult or unpleasant thing

resonate
strike a chord; ring true or familiar

reveal
show something hidden

rid
to be freed or relieved from

S

rigor

difficult, severe, or strict

rigorous

extremely detailed, involved, or accurate

salient

most important or noticeable

scholar

student or learner

scope

extent of something

secondary

coming after something more important

secure

obtain; get a hold of

selective

choosing carefully

self-advocate

publicly support yourself

semester

half-year term in a school or college

shore

improve or strengthen

socioeconomic

related to social and economic factors

sophisticated

modern, up to date

standards

rules for measuring or evaluating

steadfast
determined, firm and unwavering

stimulate
draw attention or interest

suffice
enough, adequate

sum
add

supplemental
in addition, extra

T

thorough
looking at every detail carefully and completely

thus
as a result; as a consequence

totality
the whole

traditional
habitually done; long-established

transition
changing from one state or position to another

U

ultimately
at the most basic level

underrepresented
not enough visibility in society

unenviable
difficult, undesirable, or unpleasant

unfathomable
not able to be fully explored or understood

uniformity

consistent, conforming to the same standard

unique

unlike anything else; the only one of its kind

vibrant

full of energy and enthusiasm

violate

break a rule

vague

not certain or clear

variety

different types

vast

having a great quantity, immense

vexing

causing annoyance, frustration, or worry

vibrant

full of energy and enthusiasm

virtually

nearly, almost

vital

absolutely necessary or important, essential

vocational

relating to an occupation or employment

voraciously

having a large appetite; excessively eager

vouching

confirming that something is true or accurate

W

willingly
readily; of one's own free will

Made in USA - Kendallville, IN
35492_9781948846707
10.14.2022 1305